ROOKERY

ROOKERY NOOK

A Farce in Three Acts

BY

BEN TRAVERS

SAMUEL FRENCH

LONDON

NEW YORK TORONTO SYDNEY HOLLYWOOD

ISBN 0 573 01389 6

This play was produced on June 30, 1926, at the Aldwych Theatre, London, with the following cast:

GERTRUDE TWINE . .	Miss Ethel Coleridge.
MRS. LEVERETT . .	Miss Mary Brough.
HAROLD TWINE . .	Mr. J. Robertson Hare.
CLIVE POPKISS . . .	Mr. Tom Walls.
GERALD POPKISS . .	Mr. Ralph Lynn.
RHODA MARLEY. . .	Miss Winifred Shotter.
PUTZ.	Mr. Griffith Humphreys.
ADMIRAL JUDDY . .	Mr. Gordon James.
POPPY DICKEY . . .	Miss Ena Mason.
CLARA POPKISS . . .	Miss Stella Bonheur.
MRS. POSSETT . . .	Miss Vera Gerald.

CHARACTERS

Gertrude Twine.
Mrs. Leverett.
Harold Twine.
Clive Popkiss.
Gerald Popkiss.
Rhoda Marley.
Pütz.
Admiral Juddy.
Poppy Dickey.
Clara Popkiss.
Mrs. Possett.

The Action takes place in the lounge-hall of "Rookery Nook," Chumpton-on-Sea, Somerset. It begins on a night in Summer.

ROOKERY NOOK

ACT 1

SCENE: *The lounge-hall of "Rookery Nook" is in darkness as it is late on a summer night. There is a trace of daylight left, and as the front door stands open facing the audience* R. C. *of the back wall, the shrubbery across the drive can be faintly seen. As the Act progresses the moon rises. From the hall the staircase runs up* L. *and the balcony for landing in each case is seen. On this balcony is a door* L. *(and, if the balance and appearance of the set requires a second opening, that which leads to the back stairs which are not shown.) The balcony runs off the set* R. *and* L. *On the* R. *there are two doors which lead to other bedrooms. On the ground floor are two doors on each side of the hall. These, as explained later, lead* R. *to drawing-room and study,* L. *to kitchen quarters and dining-room. The electric light switches operating the hall lights are just inside the door,* D. L. *The hall is well furnished with a very fine hall table slightly* R. *of* C., *a Chesterfield sofa and hall chairs. A parquet floor with rugs: in the back wall are large windows.*

(GERTRUDE TWINE *discovered* C. *above table.*)

GERTRUDE. Mrs. Leverett! (*Raps on table.*) Mrs. Leverett! (*No answer. She is a woman in the thirties, a critical, suspicious type of seaside resident. She is in semi-evening dress with a wrap. Calls again.*) Mrs. Leverett!

MRS. LEVERETT. (*Heard off.*) Oh, is that Mrs. Twine? Very good; I'll come.

(GERTRUDE C. MRS. LEVERETT *enters from down left. She is a stout person wearing a striking tartan blouse, tweed skirt and no hat; leaves door open through which a strong light shows through.*)

GERTRUDE. Hasn't he arrived? (*Moves to* MRS. LEVERETT.)

MRS. LEVERETT. (*Querulously.*) No, he has not, Mrs. Twine, and look at the time. I may say I was engaged by the day and not by the night.

GERTRUDE. (*Freezingly.*) All right, all right. "Has he arrived?—*No.*" That's all I wanted. *No.*

MRS. LEVERETT. (*Getting rattled.*) I suppose there is no question he *is* coming to-night?

GERTRUDE. Of course he is. That's why you're waiting here.

MRS. LEVERETT. Yes, but I should never have consented to wait had I known he was going to keep me here at improper hours. (*Cross* L., *switch on lights.*)

GERTRUDE. You must make allowances. In the ordinary way the whole party would have been here by this time.

MRS. LEVERETT. H'm. I prefer to work for parties of regular habits.

(*Waves imaginary cat away into kitchen and closes door.*)

(*This fires* GERTRUDE. *A breeze springs up.*)

GERTRUDE. My sister is a most considerate person. Was it *her* fault that my mother was taken ill at the last moment? (*Crosses* L. *of table to front.*)

MRS. LEVERETT. I'm not saying—(*Crosses to* GERTRUDE L. C.)

GERTRUDE. And couldn't be brought here?

MRS. LEVERETT. I know, madam, but—I can't worry about their troubles.

GERTRUDE. Don't talk like that of your betters, please.

MRS. LEVERETT. I'm not talking like that of my betters.

GERTRUDE. Yes, you are. (*Slight pause as they glare at each other.*) My sister did the only possible thing—stayed and looked after my mother. (*Crosses to front of table.*)

MRS. LEVERETT. Madam! I am not making any complaint about your sister. But her husband was coming here alone——

GERTRUDE. It isn't "he *was* coming." He *is* coming.

MRS. LEVERETT. When?

GERTRUDE. I only know he's coming to-night. (*This as if trying to drum home a thing for the twentieth time.*)

MRS. LEVERETT. Yes, but *when* to-night?

GERTRUDE. Oh, how can I tell? (*Breaking off*

with a little " t'ck " of annoyance, cross R. *in front of table.*) When a man gets left alone with a car, there's always trouble. If the car doesn't go wrong, the man does.

MRS. LEVERETT. (*Much more patiently.*) Well, excuse me (*cross* D. L. *and come back*), but can't you wait here for him, madam ? Or can't Mr. Twine ?

TWINE. (*Appearing at front door.*) Yes. Hallo ! What's that ?

(TWINE *is a short, feeble man of about forty in a dinner suit and straw hat.*)

GERTRUDE. Oh, there you are, Harold.

TWINE. (*Coming down.*) Yes, dear.

GERTRUDE. Gerald hasn't arrived.

TWINE. No, dear.

GERTRUDE. How did you know ?

TWINE. I didn't, dear.

GERTRUDE. Then why say " no " like that ?

TWINE. Like what, dear ?

GERTRUDE. Is Clive there ?

TWINE. Yes, dear.

GERTRUDE. Call him in.

TWINE. Yes, dear. (*Crosses to door—at door* R. C. *calling.*) Clave ! Clave !

GERTRUDE. Where is he ?

TWINE. (*Calling.*) Clave ! Clave !

GERTRUDE. Clive !

TWINE. Clave !

CLIVE. (*Appearing at front door.*) All right ; don't make an anthem of it.

(CLIVE *is a sport in the thirties. He wears a dinner suit.*)

(TWINE *crosses* L. *to* MRS. LEVERETT, *and she tells him her troubles as* CLIVE *comes down* R. C. *to* GERTRUDE.)

GERTRUDE. Come in. Come in.

CLIVE. Oh, so this is the house you've got for them, is it? What a nice house! Nice, peaceful atmosphere for a change.

GERTRUDE. What do you mean—for a change?

CLIVE. For them. For Gerald and Clara. They're coming here, aren't they?

GERTRUDE. I don't see why you should say they want a peaceful atmosphere for a *change*. They've only been married six weeks.

CLIVE. I don't mean that.

	GERTRUDE	
CLIVE	C.	TWINE
R. C.		L. C.
		MRS. LEVERETT
		L.

GERTRUDE. Well, what *do* you mean?

CLIVE. (*Long-suffering, stifling his impatience.*) They're on a holiday, aren't they?

GERTRUDE. Well?

CLIVE. Just like I'm on a holiday—(*cross to* GERTRUDE)—staying with *you*.

GERTRUDE. Well?

CLIVE. Yes—well, I say—what a nice house they're coming to. Lucky people.

GERTRUDE. (*A little jealous.*) Haven't you come to a nice house? Isn't mine nice?

CLIVE. (*Getting past his patience.*) Oh, very. There can be two nice houses, can't there?

Gertrude. (*Who shines at female argument.*) You don't suppose I'd have got them a house that *wasn't* nice (*turning away* L.), do you ?

Clive. (*Turning, cross* D. R. *desperately, speaking to himself.*) Oh, hell !

(Twine *crosses to* Gertrude.)

Twine. Dearest !

Gertrude. What do *you* want ?

(Clive *watches them, listening.*)

Twine. It isn't I that want anything.

Gertrude. Well, who is it that wants what ?

Twine. (*Apologetically*). Mrs.—er—em——

Gertrude. Yes. I know what she wants. She wants to go home.

Mrs. Leverett. Quite right.

(Clive *moves towards* C.)

Twine. She was asking me what time I thought Gerald would arrive.

Gertrude. (*Very annoyed.*) Well, gracious me, how can I tell ? I've been asked that twenty times. Don't ask me again.

Twine. (*Very subdued.*) He only had to come on from your mother's at Bath. Bath isn't far—a matter of two hours. He ought to have started——

Gertrude. Started ! He ought to have been here hours ago.

(Twine *goes up* L.)

Mrs. Leverett. Well, something's got to be done about it.

CLIVE. (*Sauntering back to* GERTRUDE C. *with malice aforethought.*) I say, Gertrude——

(*Table.*)

		TWINE	
CLIVE	GERTRUDE	L. C.	(*Settee.*)
R. C.	C.		
		MRS. LEVERETT	
		L.	

CLIVE. (*Airily, crosses to* GERTRUDE.) About what time do you suppose old Gerald will breeze along?

GERTRUDE. Clive, you're trying to annoy me.

CLIVE. (*With injured innocence.*) Annoy you, Gertrude? I like that. I wouldn't do such a thing. I was going to suggest something.

GERTRUDE. I shouldn't think *that* would be likely to help.

CLIVE. Oh, all right. I was only going to suggest a suggestion. (*He crosses* L. C. *to* MRS. LEVERETT.) P'r'aps *you* might like to hear it. It's really a good one.

MRS. LEVERETT. I have no time to listen, sir. I must be *off*.

CLIVE. Oh, don't be that.

MRS. LEVERETT. If you knew in what a hurry I was to get home, sir, you'd offer to wait here yourself for the coming gentleman.

CLIVE. You must be psychic.

MRS. LEVERETT. (*Obviously shocked.*) I *beg* your pardon—I'm nothing of the kind.

CLIVE. We've got the same idea. (*Turning to* GERTRUDE.) There you are. We've fixed it. I'll stay here till Gerald comes, and Mrs. Flannelfoot will waddle off home.

Gertrude. (*Considering this.*) Oh—I see.

Mrs. Leverett. (*Briskly.*) If the gentleman is willing, that settles it. I'll get me hat. (*Goes off* D. L.)

(Twine *comes down* L. C.)

Gertrude. Oh, well, if you're going to be left here alone, I hope you're to be trusted. You'll be responsible for the house, not only to Gerald, but also to the Mantle Hams.

Clive. (*Cross to* Gertrude.) To the who?

Gertrude. The Mantle Hams. The people this house belongs to.

Clive. Oh, the Mantle Hams. That's a good one. But I fail to see what trouble I can get into here alone for a few minutes. (*Sits on table* C.) If you can think of any, I wish you'd let me know.

Gertrude. (*Decisively.*) Someone's got to hang about here, so I suppose you'd better.

Clive. Righto then. I'm very good at hanging about.

Twine. (*Tentatively.*) Erm——

Clive. (*Looking at* Twine *curiously.*) Yes?

Twine. (*Looking at* Gertrude.) Erm——

Gertrude. (*Who has turned towards door, looking round again.*) Well, what's the matter?

Clive. Shh! Don't discourage him. I think Harold is going to lay an egg.

Gertrude. Clive, don't be coarse.

Twine. No, I only thought——

Gertrude. You thought what?

TWINE. Wouldn't it be as well for me to stay as well?

GERTRUDE. What?

CLIVE. Now, old sportsman, sort yourself. (*Patting him gently.*)

TWINE. (*Precisely.*) Shall I stay too?

CLIVE. No.

GERTRUDE. No.

CLIVE. Carried.

GERTRUDE. Why do you want to stay?

TWINE. I don't, dear.

GERTRUDE. Then why say you did?

TWINE. I didn't mean I did. I meant if you'd rather I did, should I?

CLIVE. The answer is a sponge cake.

GERTRUDE. Oh, come home. (*Cross* U. R.)

TWINE. Yes, dear.

(CLIVE *trips him playfully as he crosses.*)

(*Apologises.*) I'm sorry.

CLIVE. Oh, it's all right.

(GERTRUDE *turns back;* TWINE *is following close on her heels: he drops down* R. *and starts to nibble his straw hat.*)

GERTRUDE. (*To* CLIVE.) Let me know directly Gerald arrives. I've got several things to see to at home, or I'd wait myself. Tell him I may be able to come over and see him later.

CLIVE. That'll amuse him.

GERTRUDE. What?

CLIVE. Oh, nothing.

GERTRUDE. (*Is going.*) Harold! Don't stand

there nibbling your straw hat. I'm always telling you about that. Put it on your head.

TWINE. Yes, dear. (D. R.)

(*The* TWINES *depart up* R.)

CLIVE. And those whom the gods love die young.

(*He gives an elaborate gesture of pent-up fury. Then he turns and crosses to the door* D. L., *which he opens.*)

I say, you haven't gone—— ?

(*The noise of a cat is heard. He steps back quickly.*)

Oh, sorry.

(*He steps out again into the hall.* MRS. LEVERETT, *now wearing a hat, follows him.*)

MRS. LEVERETT. Was that you, sir ?

CLIVE. Yes.

(MRS. LEVERETT *shoos cat away, and shuts door* D. L.)

I'm afraid I trod on the cat. (*Cross* L. C.)

MRS. LEVERETT. Then kindly do not do so.

CLIVE. Ah, too late. I've done it now. (*Up* L. C.)

MRS. LEVERETT. You know this gentleman, I take it ?

CLIVE. Who ? Mr. Popkiss ? (*Behind table* C.)

MRS. LEVERETT. Yes. The one that's expected.

CLIVE. Oh, rather. He's my cousin. My name's Popkiss, too.

MRS. LEVERETT Oh, I see. Then you're also related to Mrs. Twine ?

CLIVE. No, that I'm not. He's my cousin and he married Mrs. Twine's sister ; that's all.

MRS. LEVERETT. Oh, is that all?

CLIVE. Yes, quite enough. And Mrs. Twine (*cross back of table to* R. *and looks at knick-knacks on the desk*) very, very kindly invited me to stay down here. And knowing my cousin was coming here, I like a fool fell for it.

MRS. LEVERETT. (*Cross* R. *to* CLIVE.) Oh! Yes, I know Mrs. Twine's house well enough—Frascati. A very nice house.

CLIVE. Personally, I'd much rather be in this one. (*Cross* D. R.)

MRS. LEVERETT. (*Betrayed from her hurry into the love of gossip, cross* R.) Yes? Well, this house—Rookery Nook—now, I reckon it's in the wrong part of Chumpton.

CLIVE. Not for me.

MRS. LEVERETT. I mean, this here Lighthouse Road don't lead anywhere.

CLIVE. No, I've noticed that. (*Cross in front of table* C., *sits.*) Not even to the lighthouse. But *all* this place is exceedingly quiet. There's nothing doing—you know what I mean—no amusement—no fun.

MRS. LEVERETT. (*Cross to table.*) No. I'm glad to say Chumpton is a very respectable place—for the *most* part.

CLIVE. In which direction lies the *least* part?

MRS. LEVERETT. Though I suppose every place has its black mark. (*Cross to* L. *of table.*) Well, I must really be getting home, sir.

CLIVE. I say, where is the black mark here?

MRS. LEVERETT. (*Again lured into gossip, crosses to* CLIVE, *returning in a more confidential manner.*) Well, sir, just what I was saying about this particular part of the place—one of these houses nearby here, for instance, has a most improper reputation.

CLIVE. No?

MRS. LEVERETT. Yes.

CLIVE. (*With interest.*) Really! Oh, go on. Where and what?

MRS. LEVERETT. Meself I wonder Chumpton puts up with it. A foreigner living here, with a step-daughter. So-called. Huh!

CLIVE. Oh? And—isn't she really his step-daughter?

MRS. LEVERETT. (*Decidedly.*) No, sir.

(*Warning for car.*)

CLIVE. How do you know?

MRS. LEVERETT. Well, Mrs. Twine knows most things.

CLIVE. You're quite right, she does.

MRS. LEVERETT. And her cook told me that the story of the step-daughter was all sheer hullaballoo.

CLIVE. Is that so?

MRS. LEVERETT. Yes. Well, the very name of the house is enough. Malmaison Cottage. And you, sir, being a scholar, will know that that is French, and *means* "a bad house."

CLIVE. I see, a sort of advertisement on the gate.

MRS. LEVERETT. Yes. And now, sir, reely, I must hurry away. (*Cross* L.)

CLIVE. What, again? All right. Off you trot.

MRS. LEVERETT. (*Cross* L. C.) Mind you, I

don't actually know these persons. At least, I know them both by sight very well, but that's all. And that's enough, seeing he's a foreigner and she as good English as what I am.

Clive. Yes. But she might still be his *step*-daughter.

Mrs. Leverett. Why, sir?

Clive. Her being English wouldn't stop her being his *step*-daughter.

Mrs. Leverett. Oh! Then all I can say is it's a very slippery step. Now, sir, if you please. I cannot remain and let you talk to me any longer.

Clive. Quite right. We must be careful, or Mrs. Twine will be saying things about *us.* (*Pushes* Mrs. Leverett *playfully*—l.—*goes up towards door* r. *At front door looking off* l. *hears a motor-horn and sees reflection of car lights through window, with sudden exclamation.*) Hallo! Wait a minute; here is my cousin.

Mrs. Leverett. (*Pausing.*) At last.

Clive. I'll go and help him.

(Gerald *is seen driving the car past the windows from* l. *to* r.)

Mrs. Leverett. (*Cross* r., *going to door.*) The garridge doors is open. (*Cross to* l. c.)

(*The car is heard to stop.*)

(Mrs. Leverett *comes* c. *and stands facing door.*)

(Gerald *enters, a young, smiling, and cheerful man, in travelling outfit, and carrying a handbag and light overcoat. He wears a cap.*)

Gerald. (*Taking his cap off.*) Rookery Nook?

Mrs. Leverett. (*Snappily.*) Yes.

Gerald. (*Putting down bag.*) Good. I'm coming here.

Mrs. Leverett. You've bin coming for some time.

Gerald. A month. I was told I should be met by a daily woman. Are you it—the daily woman?

Mrs. Leverett. (*With a sniff.*) H'm. I'm not so sure that I *am* now.

Gerald. Well, perhaps you could find out. (*Puts bag on table.*)

Mrs. Leverett. I am a working wife and mother, and there at home waiting for me is my five children and cetera, not to mention my husband and what not.

Gerald. Oh, you've got five children and a what-not—I wonder you can find time to be a daily.

Mrs. Leverett. 'Owever, now you have come, I may as well show you the house and quit.

Gerald. Where's the quit?

Mrs. Leverett. Quit. Go. I'll go.

Gerald. Oh, go. You'll go. Good! Yes, thanks very much. I see. Quit—I thought you meant the quit was some sort of—well, I mean, quit—it might be anything.

Mrs. Leverett. Well, this is the main 'all.

Gerald. Oh, that is the main hall, is it?

Mrs. Leverett. (*Cross up* L.) This is the dining-room. (*Indicating off up* L.) I suppose you've had all the food you need to-night.

Gerald. Yes, I had something on the way.

MRS. LEVERETT. Yes, I should think you *did.* (*Indicating off* L.) The dining-room.

GERALD. (*Looking in.*) Oh, a nice square room; thanks very much.

(CLIVE *enters* R. C.)

CLIVE. I say, Gerald, you didn't leave me out there with the idea that I was going to wash the car and put it away for you, did you?

GERALD. No. Have you unstrapped the trunks?

CLIVE. Yes, I've done that.

(MRS. LEVERETT *crosses to study door* D. R., *which she opens. Throughout this scene she hustles* GERALD *unwillingly from room to room.*)

MRS. LEVERETT. The study! (*Impatiently.*)

(CLIVE *crosses to back of table.*)

GERALD. (*Turning to study.*) The study? That's very nice. (*To* CLIVE.) We might go and sit in there——

MRS. LEVERETT. (*Closing study door.*) I can't sit anywhere.

GERALD. Why, what have you done to yourself?

MRS. LEVERETT. (*Looking fiercely at* GERALD *and crossing up* R., *opening drawing-room door and immediately closing it again.*) Mrs. Mantle Ham's drawing-room.

(CLIVE *crosses to* R. *front of table.*)

GERALD. Oh! (*She closes door.*) Very nice outside.

MRS. LEVERETT. (*Cross* L. *in front of settee,*

followed by Gerald ; *opens kitchen door* d. l.) The kitchen and so on. Those are my quarters. You don't want to see them, do you ?

Gerald. (*To* Clive.) I don't think we want to see her quarters, do we ? No, we won't.

Mrs. Leverett. (*Pointing up* r.) The stairs.

Gerald. Oh, impossible !

Mrs. Leverett. The door there is the main bedroom. The bed is made. The bathroom is next door. The other bedrooms is elsewhere.

Gerald. (*To* Clive.) I wonder who thought of that.

Mrs. Leverett. (*Crosses to kitchen.*) I must get back now hurried. (*Crosses to* Gerald.) Oh, here is the front-door key. I have the back. I will come at eight-thirty in the morning. Earlier than that I cannot be. And good night to you. (*Turns towards kitchen door.*)

Gerald. Yes ; but, I say, hold on one moment.

Mrs. Leverett. What, sir ? Quickly, please.

Gerald. There were just one or two things I wanted to ask you.

Mrs. Leverett. What was it you wanted to know, please ?

Gerald. It's all right. Only I thought there were to be some other girls here besides you. You know—maids.

Mrs. Leverett. Ah ! (*Cross to* Gerald.) But not yet, sir. Mrs. Twine put them off directly she heard you were coming alone.

Gerald. Why ? (Mrs. Leverett *gives an elaborate shrug.*) Oh, I see. (*To* Clive.) You hear that ?

Mrs. Leverett. Good night then. And eight-thirty in the morning. (*Cross* L. *at kitchen door.*) Oh, and there is also a cat. It lives in the kitchen. (*Coming back* L. C.)

Gerald. It had better.

Mrs. Leverett. Kindly mind out for it. It's been trod on once to-night already (*looks at* Clive *freezingly*) even in there.

(*She goes off* D. L., *closing door.*)

Gerald. Well, here we are. It was very nice of you to be over here to meet me, old boy.

Clive. You needn't flatter yourself. I only stayed over here away from those blasted Twines.

Gerald. (*Laughs.*) Yes, I wanted you there.

Clive. Dash it, what have I ever done to you?

Gerald. I wanted *you* there, so that I shouldn't have to go about with Harold.

Clive. Well, anyway, I'm very glad you've come.

Gerald. Yes, and I'm very glad you're here. You can help me in with my portmanteau. (*Cross* R. *back of table.*)

Clive. Oh, hell! is it heavy?

Gerald. Yes, it is very. Come on, old boy. (*Going to door.*)

Clive. (*Going reluctantly up* R. C.) All right. If I'd only known, I'd have had Twine over to do it.

(*They go out* R. C. *together and can be heard getting the portmanteau off the car.*)

Gerald. (*Off.*) Stand there. I'll give it a heave.

CLIVE. All right. Go on then. You go first. You can be the one to go backwards.

(They reappear carrying the portmanteau, GERALD *walking backwards.)*

GERALD. (R. C., *looking up* L. *over his shoulder.)* I suppose that's my room.

CLIVE. I don't care. I'm not going to carry it upstairs.

GERALD. Righto. Put it down.

(They put it down up stage L. C.*)*

CLIVE. Too hot for that stuff.

GERALD. Yes. You're quite right. We ought to have had Harold.

CLIVE. I suppose you've got a bottle in it ?

GERALD. That's in that one. *(Indicating suitcase* R.*)*

CLIVE. *(Cross* R. *to suitcase on table.)* Then why not say so ? We need never have got the portmanteau.

(He opens suitcase ; pushes several miscellaneous contents out on to the floor, handkerchiefs, etc.)

GERALD. I say, Clive, careful, old boy.

CLIVE. *(Picking things up.)* I'm sorry, but you had to unpack, didn't you ?

GERALD. *(Taking whisky bottle from the suitcase.)* There you are, old boy. *(Handing it to* CLIVE.*)* Shall I get some glasses ? *(Goes to kitchen.)*

CLIVE. Yes, I hate drinking out of the bottle !

GERALD. I'll get some glasses. *(Opens door*

down R. *and bus. driving imaginary cat away.)* Go out—I mean—don't do that—stay in—Pss!

CLIVE. What's up?

GERALD. *(Off.)* Cat.

CLIVE. Did you tread on it?

GERALD. No, I missed it.

CLIVE. Oh, pity. *(Puts bag back* R. *and comes back to table* C.) And see if that fellow left any soda.

GERALD. What fellow?

CLIVE. The owner of the house. You know—Brindle Stag or whatever his damn silly name is.

GERALD. Yes. Oh, here's some water. I'd better bring that.

(He returns, carrying two glasses and jug of water. Kicks backward to scare the cat and shuts the door with his foot.)

Get back there—shoo! I hate cats!

CLIVE. That's better. *(Leaves* GERALD *to mix drinks at table and strolls over* L.) Ye gods, if you knew what it was like over at those two teetotal Twines'!

GERALD. *(Pouring whiskies, one strong, one weak.)* Well, think of me, old boy. I've got Gertrude permanently as a sister-in-law. How different from dear little Clara! Queer thing that—two sisters so unlike.

CLIVE. *(Looking at the drinks.)* Gerald, which of these is mine?

GERALD. Just as you like. *(Looks carefully at drinks.)* Take that one. *(Pushes small one to* CLIVE*—turns to portmanteau.)*

*(*CLIVE *changes tumblers.* GERALD *sees him.* GERALD *returns from portmanteau to*

re-change tumblers. Meanwhile these lines are spoken.)

Clive. Righto. Shall I do this for you? (*With water jug.*)

Gerald. Yes, please.

(Clive *pours water in each glass and changes them again, taking the strong one.*)

Clive. Yes, poor little Twine. At times he must long for death—probably Gertrude's.

(Gerald *tastes drink, takes more whisky.*)

What's the matter—too strong?

Gerald. Not yet. I'm afraid Harold will never assault Gertrude. (*Crosses to* L. *front of table.*)

Clive. No. I might. (*Crosses to* R. *front of table.*) Poor little Twine. The way she dosses him up, and makes him trot about after her, wearing his little straw hat and looking like a rabbit at a stoat's tea party!

Gerald. Well, you'll have me and Clara here now. (*Crosses to portmanteau.*)

Clive. When's Clara coming? (*Crosses behind table.*)

Gerald. (*Returning to his unpacking.*) Oh, she'll bring the old woman along pretty soon. (*Places ties on table* C.)

(*Bus.* Clive *walks with* Gerald *each time backwards and forwards, getting in his way each time.*)

Clive. What's the matter with the old woman?

Gerald. I don't know. (*Pushes* Clive *gently.*) She didn't say much. (*Putting bottle encased in wood with screw top on table, also pyjamas and loofah on table* C. *front.*)

CLIVE. Didn't she? That sounds as if she were dying. (*Getting between* GERALD *and table.*) Well, couldn't we wangle that I come and put up here with you? (*At portmanteau* L.)

GERALD. I don't know, old boy. Rather impossible if you're staying with Gertrude. Clara might be able to get you over. (*Crossing to table with bath gown.*)

(CLIVE *is standing in his way.*)

Get out of the way, old boy. (*Pushing him.*)

CLIVE. Couldn't I stay here now—I mean—before Clara comes? (*Has picked up a tie and is toying with it.*) How do you do these things?

(GERALD *takes it and pushes him gently away.*)

I mean you do want me here, don't you?

GERALD. Do I? (*Going to portmanteau.*)

CLIVE. If you only knew what I've suffered at the hands of those relations of yours.

GERALD. It doesn't worry me. I'm not there.

(*Bus.* CLIVE *is now toying with a screw stopper on bottle.*)

(*Taking it from him.*) Don't do that, old boy; if you want to play with one of these, that's the place to get them. (*Pointing at name.*) The name's at the bottom. (*Crosses to portmanteau and brings other things back.*)

(*By this time* CLIVE *has picked up a bath gown.*)

(*Taking it from him.*) Don't mess that gown about, old boy, you'll get it all creased.

Clive. It's a lovely colour.

Gerald. Yes. All the more reason not to mess it about.

Clive. Well, what am I to do?

Gerald. You must find something else to do. This is my favourite garment. I'm very fond of that.

Clive. I mean about getting away from Gertrude's. (*Crosses* R. C. *to* R. *front of table.*)

Gerald. You can't; that's all.

Clive. (*Strolling round* R. *of table to front.*) No, I suppose not. After all, I suppose when you've been married six weeks you don't want other people knocking around all the time.

Gerald. (*Coming round* L. *of table to front, grins.*) Very little of the time.

Clive. How's it going? (*Sitting on table.*)

Gerald. Marriage? Oh, fine, old boy.

Clive. A veil is drawn over the past, eh?

Gerald. What do you mean?

Clive. (*Taking whisky.*) Well, dash it, we had a few bright adventures in our time, didn't we?

Gerald. Oh, a veil. Yes, a very thick veil. (Clive *pours out whisky.*) You'll help yourself, won't you?

Clive. Yes, I will, old boy. Do you remember——

Gerald. (*Quickly.*) No, I don't. And look here, I say, Clive—while you're staying in this place—I mean with the relations here and that sort of thing—don't go and get into trouble, will you? You know what I mean—with anything *local*.

Clive. You needn't be afraid. There's nothing to be found in this place.

GERALD. How do you know?

CLIVE. I've been here a whole week and drawn a complete blank. There's nothing here at all.

GERALD. Oh, that's a pity.

CLIVE. Yes. Well, I suppose we shall have to play golf, that's all.

GERALD. Don't give up hope. We thought we were going to play golf that time at Bognor, d'you remember?

CLIVE. Oh yes. That was the time we met—Annie and Winnie.

GERALD. Oh, Annie and Winnie. Yes. What a memory you've got! Annie was the stout one and Winnie was the pretty one.

CLIVE. Yes.

GERALD. You, you old devil, you pinched Winnie.

CLIVE. Oh, I pinched old Annie too.

(*Warning—distant door bang and short bark of dog*—O. P.)

GERALD. Well, as I say, old boy, none of that Annie and Winnie stuff this time.

CLIVE. As I say you needn't worry, there's nothing here at all. Gertrude only lives in this place because here she's comparatively good-looking.

GERALD. Of course, so far the only one I've seen is the daily one. And she looks like a non-swimmer in deep water.

CLIVE. You've only got to look at this place. (*Cross* R. C.) Look at it now. Only just dark and you can hear the silence.

Gerald. Yes. (*Cross to* Clive.)

Bang.

(*Dog and bang of door in distance.*)

Clive. What was that ?

Gerald. A dog, I think.

Clive. Yes, but there was a sort of bang.

Gerald. Oh, then perhaps somebody shot the dog.

Clive. It sounded more like a door bang.

Gerald. Somebody letting out the dog.

Clive. Why should he bang the door like that ?

Gerald. He probably ought to have let the dog out sooner. (*Pause.*) You can't see anything from there, can you ?

Clive. Well, you don't want to see a dog being let out. Now are you going to start clearing up this ghastly mess ?

Gerald. I haven't begun yet. I've more things in the car. (*Turns.*)

Clive. Well, you'd better hurry up or you'll have Gertrude round.

Gerald. Why, she's not coming over, is she ?

Clive. You bet she is—she'll come along, nosing about like an old hen that's had her run dug up. (*Flapping his arms and scratching with his foot as a hen.*)

Gerald. Well, go and tell her I haven't arrived.

Clive. But, you silly old fat-head, I've only been left here till you did.

Gerald. Oh, I see. Well, tell her I'm too tired.

Clive. All right. I'll do my best, and then

come back. Don't take that up to your bedroom. (*Indicating whisky. Turns towards door* R. C.)

GERALD. If you're coming back, there won't be any to take.

CLIVE. Well, I'll try and put the lid on Gertrude.

GERALD. And Harold.

CLIVE. If I get the lid on, he can sit on it.

(*Exit up* R.)

(GERALD *tidies the table and looks about for something in his portmanteau* L., *and goes out* R. C.)

(*The figure of* RHODA, *a young and very pretty girl in pink silk pyjamas, passes window* L., *just glancing in. She then comes to door* R., *pauses, looks round, crosses to* L. *in front of table, looks up to balcony* L., *then sees bath gown on table* C. *and sits on table drying her feet with the bath gown; she is facing half* L.)

(GERALD *returns with a case and golf clubs; he puts them down* R., *clubs* R. *of case; he sees her, then picks up bag and clubs, goes out again to make certain he's made no mistake about the house. He comes back, puts things down again, looking at her in a dazed way, shutting and opening his eyes. He then goes to the door* R. C., *calling helplessly.*)

GERALD. Clive!

RHODA. (*As she turns and sees him.*) Oh! Er—is this your house?

GERALD. Yes, I think so.

RHODA. I mean, you've just got here, or something?

GERALD. Yes, but haven't you, or something?

RHODA. Yes. My name's Rhoda Marley. I come from up the road. I live there with my step-father.

GERALD. Oh, did you?—I mean, do you? Is he ill, or is your house on fire?

RHODA. No. It's nothing like that, but—shall I tell you?

GERALD. (*Getting closer.*) Yes, please, I wish you would.

RHODA. Oh, thank you. Only—excuse me a moment.

(*She shifts her sitting position and extracts a loofah. She smiles half-bashfully.*)

It was pricking me rather.

GERALD. Oh, was it? It should only scratch. Hadn't you better sit on something softer?

RHODA. I sat up here to dry my feet. I had to come through some very long grass to get here.

GERALD. Yes, I see—the ends of your——

RHODA. Pyjama trousers——

GERALD. Pyjama trousers—oh yes, I couldn't remember the name.

RHODA. Yes, I know. They're very damp too. There's a heavy dew, you see.

GERALD. Yes. I can see there is. (*Getting closer.*) Still, it's supposed to be a sign of fine weather, isn't it?

RHODA. Yes. (*Embarrassed pause.*) Well, I'd better tell you why I've come.

GERALD. Do, will you, please?

RHODA. Well, it's rather a long story.

GERALD. Oh, it can't be. I mean, here you are in pyjamas on my table.

(RHODA *slips off table.*)

Oh, that's all right. But why? That's all—why?

RHODA. (*Appealingly.*) It's all quite harmless. But I'm in such trouble. Oh, please, do be kind to me.

GERALD. (*Softening.*) Kind to you? I'd do anything. But that's just it. What do you want me to do?

RHODA. Well, first of all—could you lend me a dressing-gown?

GERALD. Oh yes—(*doubtfully*)—a dressing-gown? Certainly. (*Cross up* L., *pulling dressing-gown from trunk and holding it up for her.*) Here you are. This one's rather shot.

RHODA. (*Notices pyjamas on table, getting into dressing-gown.*) Thanks awfully. I'm afraid I've rather spoilt that bath wrap.

GERALD. Oh, never mind about that rotten old thing. (*Throwing it down and kicking it.*) Only that wasn't why you came here, to borrow a dressing-gown?

RHODA. No, I'll tell you everything. (*She shivers.*)

GERALD. You're cold. (*Nearly touches her.*)

RHODA. No, it's all right. It's only that wet grass.

GERALD. Here, drink this. (*Taking up whisky and changing it for the jug of water.*)

Rhoda. No, I don't want that.

Gerald. Well, what else can I do?

Rhoda. (*Hesitating, rubbing one leg on the other.*) I hardly like to ask. (*Smiling.*)

Gerald. Don't be afraid. What is it?

Rhoda. (*Taking a pair of his striped blue pyjama trousers from the table.*) The ends of mine have got so awfully damp.

Gerald. You—you want to put on those of mine? (*She nods.*) But—are you going to be here long?

Rhoda. Well, I'm afraid that depends on you.

Gerald. Oh, does it? Well then, you'd better put on those of mine.

Rhoda. I'm honestly in great trouble. (*In a little outburst, getting a little closer to* Gerald.) You do trust me, don't you?

Gerald. Of course. (*Making shapes with hands.*) Only can't you give me just a hint of what it's all about, before you put on my trousers?

Rhoda. I shouldn't be a minute putting them on.

Gerald. No, I don't take long putting them on —well, you'd better put them on.

Rhoda. Yes—but—— (*Looking round at door on balcony* L.)

Gerald. Oh yes. Here you are. (*Opening door* R. *and switching on light.*) The study.

Rhoda. Thanks awfully. I think you'd better shut the door.

Gerald. Oh, I was—(*holding door open* D. R.)— I'm going to shut the door.

Rhoda. No—I meant that front door.

GERALD. Oh! Why?

RHODA. You'll understand when I tell you. (*She goes into study.*)

(*He shuts study door, crosses to table, takes cigarette case from his pocket and puts cigarette in his mouth deep in thought; he takes his match-box out of his pocket, strikes a match and lights cigarette; still gazing at door* D. R., *he absent-mindedly throws cigarette away and puts the lighted match almost in his mouth. This brings him back to earth, he picks up his cigarette and starts to smoke; he looks thoughtfully straight in front and whistles quietly to himself.*)

(*From outside comes the sound of the dog barking. This is checked by a weird foreign command in the distance:* "Hoi—Na-na-na-na!" *Gerald picks up bath gown and throws it on portmanteau* L., *goes to door* R. C., *opens it. There is the sound of a blow.*)

(RHODA *enters from the study on sound of whip—blue striped pyjamas—trousers over her feet; she wears the dressing-gown. She stands just inside the hall, listens nervously.*)

(*Then the voice again:* "Zo! Na-na!"—*whip again.* GERALD *closes the front door.*)

GERALD. Are those noises anything to do with you?

RHODA. Yes (*cross to front of table nervously*); that's my step-father and his dog Conrad.

GERALD. (*Cross* C. *above table.*) Oh, really! It doesn't sound too good, does it?

Rhoda. (*Nervously.*) No, I'd better tell you everything. (*Sits on table* c.)

Gerald. Oh, don't sit on that. (*Indicating settee* l.) This is softer.

Rhoda. Thank you. (*Crosses to settee* l.)

Gerald. That's all right.

Rhoda. As I say (*sitting on back of settee*), that's my step-father ; he's a German. His name is Putz.

Gerald. Putz ! (*Sitting on settee up stage.*)

Rhoda. Yes. P–u–t–z. I live with him and a housekeeper. Her name is Nutts—Mrs. Nutts.

Gerald. Putz and Nutts ?

Rhoda. Yes.

Gerald. Is this quite true ?

Rhoda. Yes.

Gerald. Oh ! Well, go on.

Rhoda. Well, first of all, I'll tell you what's happened to-night. That's easily told. My step-father has run me out.

Gerald. What ?

Rhoda. That's his own expression for it. I annoyed him ; so just after I'd gone to bed he came up and took me up in his arms and ran me out. (*She demonstrates this with a little sound,* " Ph't ! ")

Gerald. You mean to tell me he ran you out in your pyjamas—ph't ?

Rhoda. Yes, and slammed the door on me. He wouldn't let me stay in the house any longer.

Gerald. He must be very hard to please.

Rhoda. Yes, that's his way. He makes rules, and if I disobey them that's how he treats me. He did it once before. But he came and took me back then.

GERALD. But what did you do to-night?

RHODA. Oh, nothing really. Simply a trifle. Only it was against his orders. He wouldn't have found out only Nutts split.

GERALD. But what was this forbidden thing?

RHODA. I ate wurts.

GERALD. You did what, in heaven's name?

RHODA. I ate wurts—wurtleberries—a local Somerset fruit—wurts.

GERALD. You ate wurts and Nutts split? It sounds like a fruit salad. But you mean to say that when Nutts split to Putz he ran you out for eating wurts?

RHODA. Yes. He dislikes wurts.

GERALD. Dislikes them! He must loathe the very sound of wurts! (*Goes up* C.)

RHODA. They leave a nasty stain on the face.

GERALD. You ought to have put them in your mouth.

RHODA. Well, that is all it was. He found I'd disobeyed him and eaten the forbidden fruit. So he ran me out.

GERALD. (*Closing portmanteau.*) Is he quite sane?

RHODA. Oh yes. But very Prussian and masterful.

GERALD. But why do you stay with him?

RHODA. (*Stepping off settee and cross to back of settee* D. L.) Because I promised my mother before she died that I'd stick to him.

GERALD. Not a very easy promise to keep if he runs you out.

RHODA. No. I'm through with it now. When

he recovers his temper he'll try and get me back. But I'm not *going* back this time.

GERALD. Quite right. Don't you. I never heard of such a thing. Wurts. But—but where will you go to-night ?

RHODA. (*Softly, quite genuinely at a loss.*) I don't know.

GERALD. Don't you know anyone here you can go to ?

RHODA. (*Shaking her head.*) None of the people here will have anything to do with *me*.

GERALD. Why ?

RHODA. I don't know them. Besides, one of them invented a scandalous story about me.

GERALD. (*Cross to above settee* L.) About *you*—a dear little innocent girl like you ?

RHODA. Yes. A woman here started the rumour that I wasn't really his step-daughter, but —something else.

GERALD. What woman said that ? (*Moves towards* RHODA.)

RHODA. Oh, one of these seaside residential cats.

GERALD. Was it Mrs. Twine ?

RHODA. Yes. How did you know ?

GERALD. By experience. Mrs. Twine is my sister-in-law.

RHODA. Oh, I'm sorry. (*Apologising.*)

GERALD. Oh, don't apologise. I'm delighted to hear nasty things about her. So Mrs. *Twine* said that about you, did she ? (*Crosses to front of settee.*)

RHODA. Yes. The whole place believes it now.

GERALD. Right. (*Crosses to* C.) If Mrs. Twine

said that, I'll do anything in the world to help you. There!

Rhoda. (*Crosses to* Gerald *with a little run.*) You're very kind, but if it's going to mean any bother to you——

Gerald. I don't care. Now this man Putz. You must go back there to-night, of course. But come here in the morning.

Rhoda. (*Nods, crossing to* L. C.) I'll do what you think right. I have been lucky to meet *you.* (*Moves close to* Gerald.)

Gerald. (*Smiles, pleased.*) Yes.

Rhoda. But I'll only go back there for one reason, and that's because you ask me to.

Gerald. Yes. It's very nice of you to say that about me.

Rhoda. P'r'aps he won't take me back now. (*Nervously.*)

Gerald. Oh, I'll soon see to that. I'll come over with you and talk to Mr. Putz.

(*A loud rap at the front door up* R.)

Rhoda. I think he's saved you the trouble. (*Crosses to behind settee.*)

Gerald. Wait there. I'll see. (*Cross to door* R. C., *calls.*) Who is it? (*Very nervously, but trying to put on a bold front.*)

Putz. (*Heard outside.*) Open, please.

Rhoda. Yes. That's him.

Gerald. (*She crosses up* L.) Come in. The door's not locked.

(*The door is opened, but only slightly.* Putz *enters backwards, keeping his dog out. He is a finely-built German, wearing loose cloth trousers and a white alpaca coat like a dentist.*)

PUTZ. (*To the dog, as he enters* R. C.) No, no. Hoi! Stay out from heah!

(*He gets in, closes door, turns and, taking horn-rimmed glasses from his pocket, takes stock of* GERALD. *His manner is quarrelsome. He sees* RHODA *and exclaims*:)

Ah! Alzo!

GERALD. Are you Mr. Putz?

PUTZ. You are who? (*Cross* D. R. *to* GERALD.)

GERALD. I've just been told——

PUTZ. You are who? Speak it out.

GERALD. How dare you run this girl out. Take her back at once.

PUTZ. I do not care for you.

GERALD. I don't care very much for you—take her back.

PUTZ. (*Advancing angrily, at which* GERALD *retires a little.*) You are who to say of what I shall make?

GERALD. I beg your pardon?

PUTZ. You are who——?

GERALD. Eh?

PUTZ. You are who?

GERALD. Don't bark at me like that. You ran her out in her pyjamas.

PUTZ. Vell? (*Becoming still more threatening.*)

GERALD. Vell, I mean—I mean—you mustn't do things like that. It's——

PUTZ. (*Advancing again, loudly.*) It is *vot*?

Gerald. (*Stepping away.*) Well, it's—it's very naughty.

Putz. You—are—who? (*Slowly.*)

Gerald. Yes—I—am. But I don't see it comes into it at all.

Putz. Speak!

Gerald. Dash it, I'm speaking as quick as I can. Just because she ate a few—wu——

Rhoda. (*Prompting him.*) Wurts.

Gerald. Wurts.

Putz. It is not only that she eat die vurrt. It is that she disobey me to eat die vurrt. (*Crosses door* R. C.)

Rhoda. I've had enough of your orders. I'll come back to-night and I'll leave to-morrow.

Putz. Zo? You t'ink? Eh?

Rhoda. Yes, I've kept my promise long enough. When I go, my mother's money goes with me.

Putz. (*Furious.*) Too much. You t'ink you can command me. (*Advancing towards her.*) Herr Gott! I show you——

Gerald. (*Stepping between them.*) Stop that, you rude—rude Putz. (*Takes a drink of whisky.*)

Putz. (*Challenging him, quivering.*) What you make?

Gerald. I'll show you what I make. Now, you —please—step-daughter——

Rhoda. Yes?

(Gerald *still facing* Putz. Putz *walks up and down furiously.*)

Gerald. (*Pointing to door on balcony* L.) That room up there—that's your room. The bathroom's next door and the other bedrooms is elsewhere. You'd better go up at once.

Rhoda. Very well. (*To the stairs* l.)

Gerald. If there's anything else you want, let me know.

Rhoda. Thank you.

(*Exit up stairs* l.)

(Putz *turns his head to watch her enter the room, so does* Gerald. *She goes in.*)

Gerald. (*To* Putz.) You hear that. Zo! And now I'll come to your house and get some of her clothes.

Putz. No.

Gerald. Yes. (*Leaning his elbow on table for support.*)

Putz. Nein.

Gerald. Ten.

Putz. Finish.

Gerald. Good!

Putz. If you come to my house I will call my dog and have you run out.

Gerald. If you go on like this I'll call the police and have you run in.

Putz. Nah! (*Crosses* d. r.)

(Gerald *takes another drink.*)

Gerald. (*With an effort.*) Now don't be a naughty boy. (*Going to door* r. c.) Come on.

(Putz *stays still* r. *As* Gerald *opens door* r. c., Putz *makes a sudden ejaculation to the dog outside.*)

Putz. Tzt! Putta-putta!

(*There is a sound of furious canine attack from outside.* Gerald *hastily closes the door again.*)

Gerald. I see. You have to be protected by a dog, do you?

Putz. (*Feeling his biceps.*) No, no. Also Swedish drill—first certificate. (*He starts to do Swedish drill.*) Ein, zwci, drei, vier—Frisch, from, frühlisch, frei.

Gerald. I don't care about your fried fish. Give me her clothes or I'll keep her as she is.

Putz. Das ist mir egal.

Gerald. All right——

Putz. Finish. I go.

Gerald. In that room.

Putz. Das ist mir schnuppe.

Gerald. Half in her pyjamas and half in mine.

Putz. Too much. Finish. (*Opening door.*) Und if you follow, my dog shall run you out, biting strongly. (*He goes, slamming the door behind him, shouting at dog.*)

(*Pause and bus.* Gerald *smells whisky as a tonic—cue for* Rhoda—*she opens bedroom door again.*)

Gerald. All right, he's gone; come down.

Rhoda. What happened—was he very cross? (*She comes down* l. c. *a little nervous.*)

Gerald. I ran him out; I don't mind doing that sort of thing. Do you mean to say that man is content to leave you here all night alone with a stranger?

RHODA. That's just like him. (*Leaning on table* c.) Anything rather than give way and say he was in the wrong. My poor mother used to admire it.

GERALD. Still, I don't suppose he ran your poor mother out in her nighty all over the shop.

RHODA. No, she was very happy with him.

GERALD. She wasn't, I suppose, cursed with this craving for wurts?

RHODA. She used to say he was what a man was really *meant* to be.

GERALD. That depends who meant it.

RHODA. Yes—(*pause.*)—I suppose so.

(*They both laugh with embarrassment.*)

Well, what am I to do?

GERALD. Well, I'm not quite sure. You see *we* know what's happened, and we know it's true. But I ask you, would anyone else believe it?

RHODA. But where do you think I'd better go? (*Smiling.*)

GERALD. You'd better go to bed. I don't see where else you *can* go in those.

(RHODA *crosses* L. *to stairway. She is very shy and looks round twice as she crosses.*)

Wait a minute. What are we going to do if Mrs. Twine comes back?

RHODA. Mrs. Twine—she won't come here, will she?

GERALD. She may; my cousin's coming back anyway—he's all right—but she might come back too.

RHODA. Well, couldn't I lurk somewhere? (*Looks at door* D. L.) What's in there?

GERALD. The kitchen quarters. Perhaps you could lurk in there?

RHODA. (*Opens kitchen door.*) She wouldn't come in here, would she? (*Goes in.*)

GERALD. No, I don't think so.

RHODA. (*Off* L.) There are some back stairs here.

GERALD. Well, there you are. If she goes in there you could nip up the back stairs.

RHODA. (*Returning.*) Yes, that's quite safe.

(*A knock at front door. He turns. She speaks in a whisper.*)

Is that your cousin?

GERALD. No, he'd come straight in.

RHODA. There you are then. (*Turns* L.) Kitchen, and back stairs if necessary. (GERALD *nods.*)

GERALD. You've only got one step-father, I suppose? (*She goes quietly off* L., *closing kitchen door.*)

(*Picks up bottle as protector; crosses to front door and calls:*)

Who is it?

(*No reply is heard. He opens front door. It is* TWINE.)

TWINE. (*Heartily.*) Hallo! (*Entering.*)

GERALD. No.

TWINE. Welcome to Chumpton.

GERALD. Who said so?

TWINE. Clave told us you were here.

GERALD. Where *is* Clave? (*Edging towards* L *in front of table* L.)

TWINE. Behind with Gertrude.

GERALD. But I want to go to bed.

TWINE. (*Cross* L. C. *following* GERALD.) I'm sorry. Gertrude would come. She insisted.

GERALD. Go and meet her and tell her I'm just going to bed. (*At foot of stairs.*)

TWINE. Yes, but that's just it. She wants to come and see you——

GERALD. See me going to bed?

TWINE. No. To see that you're all sort of——

GERALD. Sort of what?

TWINE. Well, sort of O.K.

GERALD. Then run quickly and meet her and tell her I am A1.

TWINE. (*Stubbornly.*) No, I don't——

GERALD. Well, I do. (*Up the stairs a little.*)

GERTRUDE. (*Off.*) Come along, Clive!

CLIVE. (*Off.*) All right.

TWINE. Here she *is.* (L. *of table* C.)

GERALD. (*Turning back into hall.*) Curse!

(GERTRUDE *enters with* CLIVE.)

(*Before looking at* GERALD, GERTRUDE *surveys the disorder of the hall with severity.* CLIVE *and* GERALD *interchange glances of protest and helplessness respectively.* GERTRUDE *catches them at it.*)

GERTRUDE. (*Cross to above table* C.) Well, this is a nice time to arrive!

GERALD. Oh, don't apologise.

GERTRUDE. You seem to have made the place in a beautiful muddle.

Gerald. Yes, that's right. I did that so that I could clear it up. (*At foot of stairs.*)

Gertrude. So this is what happens directly you get away from Clara. (*Cross* L. C. *to* Gerald.)

Gerald. What do you mean? (*Anxiously.*)

Gertrude. All this mess. (*Indicating the mess in the hall.*) Is mother very seedy? Will she and Clara be coming soon?

Gerald. I hope not.

(Twine *at back of stage, looking over* L. *shoulder at* Clive *and* Gertrude.)

Gertrude. What?

Gerald. I hope mother's not very seedy.

Gertrude. H'm! Which room are you going to? (*Looking up to balcony* L.) That double room?

Gerald. Yes, that's the one Mrs. Lightfoot said.

Twine *up.* L. C. (*Looking over* L. *shoulder with back to audience.*)

Clive	Gertrude	Gerald
R. C.	L. C.	D. L.

Gertrude. I think that room had better be left. Clara may want to sleep with mother.

Gerald. Well, I don't mind.

Gertrude. I'd better just see. (*Going upstairs.*)

Gerald. Yes.

Gertrude. Come up with me, please.

Gerald. (*Following.*) But surely I can sleep in that room *to-night*?

Gertrude. That would only give trouble,

moving your things about. (*Opens door of bedroom.*)

(Gerald *looks down at* Clive, *who is helping himself to another whisky* R. C., *and they exchange looks of sympathetic affliction.*)

Now let me see. What other rooms are there?

(*She goes towards* R., Gerald *following.*)

Twine. Can I help at all, dear? (*Standing* C., *looking up at* Gertrude.)

Gertrude. (*Going off at* R. *end of landing.*) No—stay where you are.

Gerald. (*Leaning over banisters, to* Twine.) You can move about a bit, you know.

(*She goes off* R. *of landing, followed by* Gerald.)

Gertrude. (*Off.*) Now this looks a good room. What's the matter with this?

Gerald. (*Off.*) I don't know. I haven't been in there yet.

(Twine *sits* L., *near kitchen door.* Clive *sits on table.*)

Clive. (*With a sigh—after a slight pause.*) Go on, boy, now's your chance. Have a nibble at your straw hat.

Twine. (*Who has turned his head towards kitchen door.*) Hush a moment.

Clive. What's the matter?

Twine. I thought I heard something. (*Rising.*)

Clive. (*Unexcited.*) Heard—what?

Twine. (*Cross* L. *to door* D. L. *and listening,*

looking at Clive.) I thought I heard a sort of sound.

Clive. Oh, don't be a fool, Harold.

Twine. Oh, it's a cat.

Clive. Don't you let that cat out here.

Twine. Poor thing—it's mewing.

Clive. Well, let it mew.

Twine. Perhaps it's lost its milk.

Clive. What do you mean, lost its milk?

Twine. Poor pussy! (*Opening kitchen door.*) Where are you? Come along. (*In practical tones.*) It's all right, come out.

Rhoda. (*Voice off.*) Thank goodness!

(Twine *falls back amazed.* Clive *leaps into a sitting attitude.* Rhoda *sails out into the doorway.*)

I was getting cramp. (*She sees them, claps a hand to her mouth and hurries back again, closing the door.*)

(Twine *stands back* L. C., *open-mouthed.* Clive *leaps to his feet and crosses* L. *There is a crash in the kitchen.*)

Clive. Ye gods! Where did he find that?

Twine. It's the girl from up the road.

Clive. Oh! Then me for up the road.

Gertrude. What was that noise?

(Gertrude *and* Gerald *heard up* R. Clive *closes kitchen door, turns* C.)

Clive. Not a word. On your honour, Twine Leave it to me.

Twine. All right.

(Gertrude *and* Gerald *on balcony.*)

Table.

Settee.

Twine C. Clive D. L.

(Gerald, *as he enters up* R. *and comes downstairs* L., *wildly alarmed.*)

Gerald. Well, I don't know. Stay there and I'll see.

(Gertrude *appears and follows* Gerald *down.* Clive *turns to them blandly.*)

Gertrude. What was that noise?

Clive. It's all right. It's Harold.

Gerald. But that noise?

Clive. That's right. Harold.

(Gerald *crosses to* L. *in front of settee.*)

He went in the kitchen.

Gerald. (*Alarmed.*) In the kitchen? Why?

Gertrude. Did you make that noise, Harold? (*Coming down and crossing to* C.)

Table.

Twine C. Gertrude L. C. Gerald L. Clive D. L.

Clive. Yes, he did.

Gerald. (*To* Clive.) But why did he go in the kitchen?

Clive. Good job he did. Next time he wants to make a noise like that he'd better go in the garden.

GERTRUDE. What was it? Why did you go in there, and what happened?

GERALD. (*To* CLIVE.) Leave this to me. (*Cross to* L. C.)

GERTRUDE. (*To* TWINE.) Why did you go in the kitchen?

CLIVE. I told him not to.

GERTRUDE. I'm asking *him*. (*To* TWINE.) Why did you?

TWINE. I heard a mew.

GERTRUDE. A what?

TWINE. A mew, dear. I heard mews.

CLIVE. Don't be stupid. A mew is a sort of sea-gull.

GERALD. And mews are stables.

TWINE. Well, then, a mi-ow. I heard a mi-ow.

CLIVE. Oh, don't be a baby. He heard the cat.

GERTRUDE. Did you hear the cat?

TWINE. Yes, dear.

CLIVE. He went to let the cat out.

GERALD. (*To* CLIVE.) And *did* he let the cat out?

CLIVE. (*Quickly to* GERALD.) Yes, a beauty.

GERALD. I see. He ran up against something?

CLIVE. He certainly did.

GERALD. Oh, I'd better have a look. (*Opens kitchen door and goes in, saying as he goes:*) Look out!

GERTRUDE. (*Turning* L.) What do you mean—look out?

(CLIVE *gets in front of* GERTRUDE; *they bump.*)

GERALD. I mean, look out if you're coming here. There are saucepans all over the floor.

(CLIVE *intentionally obstructs* GERTRUDE *from going into the kitchen by standing in front of the doorway looking in.*)

CLIVE. (*To* GERALD.) Is it all right?

GERALD. Yes, old boy, it's all right now.

GERTRUDE. (*Pushes past* CLIVE.) Clear out of the way. What a nuisance you are, Harold!

(*Goes in.* CLIVE *cross* C. *to* R. *of* TWINE.)

(GERALD *returns and comes hastily down to the other two.*)

GERALD. You saw? (*Confidentially.*)

CLIVE. Yes, but not long enough.

GERALD. And you saw? (*Nervously to* TWINE.)

(GERALD *takes* TWINE'S *left arm and* CLIVE *his right.*)

TWINE. Yes. (*Then the three cross* R. C. *arm-in-arm.*)

GERALD. Listen, quick! It's on the level. She was driven from home. She had to come here. But don't tell Gertrude.

CLIVE. No, no.

TWINE. Oh, I say, but——

GERALD. But nothing. As man to man—swear not to say a word.

TWINE. Oh, but it's awful.

CLIVE. It isn't.

GERALD. It isn't. Come round early to-morrow and I'll tell you all. Till then, swear!

CLIVE. Go on. Swear, blast you!

TWINE. Oh!

GERALD. You're always in the vocative. Swear!

CLIVE. Hurry up! Swear!

TWINE. Oh, botheration!

CLIVE. Not that kind of swear, you fool! Promise.

TWINE. Well, I daren't tell Gertrude that that girl's here.

GERALD. Daren't? That's all right. That's a swear. And come round in the morning early.

TWINE. But the harm will be done by then.

GERALD. Harm? There's no harm, I tell you.

CLIVE. Of course not, you evil-minded little man.

(GERTRUDE *appearing at kitchen door* D. L.)

GERTRUDE. Harold!

(CLIVE *and* GERALD *pretend to be having a joke with* TWINE.)

GERALD. Harold's just told a beauty.

TWINE. Oh, what, dear?

GERTRUDE. Are you going to leave me to pick all these things up?

TWINE. (*Cross* L. *to her.*) No, dear.

GERTRUDE. I should hope not.

(*They go, leaving kitchen door open.*)

(CLIVE *and* GERALD *cross* C.)

CLIVE. (*To* GERALD.) Now then, you naughty boy. Explain this windfall.

GERALD. A perfectly innocent, sweet little girl driven from home.

CLIVE. Go on.

GERALD. True. You wait till you see her.

CLIVE. I'm going to. But Gertrude'll see her now.

GERALD. No, she won't. She's gone up the back stairs. But you must help.

CLIVE. With pleasure.

(*Voices heard off.*)

GERALD. She's got to stay here to-night. What shall I do? I can't stay here alone with her.

CLIVE. No, you oughtn't to.

GERALD. I know. You ought to stay here too. Can't you manage it?

CLIVE. I ought to.

GERALD. You must if you can.

CLIVE. Well, you ask Gertrude.

GERALD. No, you ask her.

CLIVE. It would seem better coming from you.

GERALD. No, but you lie better than I do.

CLIVE. Do I? All right. I'll have a pop.

GERTRUDE. (*Off.*) Leave things alone.

(*Enter* D. L.)

GERALD. Go on then. Now.

(GERTRUDE *and* TWINE *reappear from kitchen. She is still upbraiding* TWINE. *Close door.*)

CLIVE. (*Cross to* GERTRUDE.) Oh, Gert—— (*Stops to look back at* GERALD, *who prods him.*)

Table.

GERALD	CLIVE		
C.	C.	GERTRUDE	TWINE
		L. C.	L.

GERTRUDE. (*Coldly.*) Gert?

GERALD. (*Aside to* CLIVE.) That's a bad start, old boy.

CLIVE. No, Gertrude. Er—we thought it

wouldn't be a bad idea if I stayed here, just for to-night, with Gerald.

Gertrude. Why?

Clive. (*To* Gerald.) Why?

Gerald. You know why, old boy. I told you.

Gertrude. Well? Why?

Gerald. (*Cross to* Gertrude.) You see—the daily woman isn't coming till eight-thirty; earlier than that she cannot be—and I oversleep—and he doesn't—do you?

Clive. Yes.

Gerald. Yes. And I want to be up early—because I want to have lunch before breakfast at seven—or half-past—well, a quarter to eight—and——

Gertrude. What are you talking about?

Gerald. Dinner. (*Crosses up* L. *of table to behind table* C.)

Clive. (*Cross to* Gertrude.) No—simply—I'd like to stay with him.

Gertrude. You're staying with me, aren't you?

Clive. Oh yes.

Gertrude. Very well then. Come along. I'm going now. (*Cross to door* R. C.) Harold!

Twine. Yes, dear.

Clive. All right then. You go ahead, you two—I'm just coming.

Gertrude. (*To* Clive.) You can catch us up. I'm not going to hang about. (*Exit* R. C.)

Gerald. (*Seizing* Twine *as he is following.*) Remember, Twine—you've sworn.

Twine. Oh, misery me!

Gerald. Haven't you?

TWINE. I'm not going to keep my mouth shut indefinitely.

CLIVE. You've sworn, until to-morrow.

TWINE. Oh-h!

GERALD. Haven't you?

TWINE. Very well. Yes.

GERTRUDE. (*Heard off.*) Harold!

CLIVE. Don't hang about. Go on.

GERALD. Go on. Get out.

(TWINE *exits up* R. C., *leaving door open.*)

(*Door open.*)

CLIVE. Well, you made a nice show of asking Gertrude.

GERALD. You said you'd ask her, and didn't.

CLIVE. How could I, when you were standing there blathering a lot of tripe about early lunch—seven-thirty—eight-fifteen?

GERALD. Well, don't blame me, and if you stay here long she may get suspicious and question Twine.

CLIVE. He won't tell.

GERALD. Don't give him the chance.

CLIVE. Dash it, he's bound to get the chance. He sleeps with her.

GERALD. Yes, poor devil!

CLIVE. Gerald, just let's have another *look*.

GERALD. All right—shut the door.

(CLIVE *shuts front door* R. C. GERALD *calls upstairs.*)

Hi! Step!

(RHODA *appears at* L. *end of landing. She is anxious again and penitent.*)

RHODA. Is it all clear now?

GERALD. Yes, she's gone.

RHODA. (*Coming downstairs* L., *pointing to door.*) I thought Mr. Twine was with you.

GERALD. Yes, but *Mrs.* didn't see you.

RHODA. *Mr.* did.

GERALD. That's all right. Don't worry. This is my cousin I told you about. Clive Popkiss—same name as me. I'm Gerald Popkiss.

CLIVE. How d'ye do?

GERALD. Very likely he'll help us to-morrow.

CLIVE. There's no very likely about it. He's going to.

RHODA. (*Who has come half-way downstairs.*) Thank you. You've been most awfully kind to me.

CLIVE. Oh, you wait until to-morrow.

GERTRUDE. (*Voice heard outside.*) Clive!

(*General scurry.* RHODA *runs up to the landing, stands at back of balcony up* L.)

CLIVE *and* GERALD. Look out! Quick! Gertrude! *etc.*

(GERTRUDE *opens front door.* RHODA *is hidden from her by the floor of the landing jutting into the hall, under which* GERTRUDE *stands.*)

GERALD. What was that you said?

CLIVE. (*Cross* R., *referring to golf bag* R.) This is a nice top.

GERTRUDE. (*To* CLIVE.) Why have you shut this door again? Will you please come along at once? (*She turns indignantly and goes out again.*)

CLIVE. Oh, sorry, Gertrude. (*Going.*) Well,

I'll have to go, old boy. (*Looks up smiling at* RHODA.) Good night, old boy.

GERALD. Good night, Clive, old boy.

(CLIVE *goes, leaving door open.*)

(CLIVE *comes back to door, looks up at* RHODA, *smiles.*)

CLIVE. Good night. (*To* GERALD.) Good night, Gerald.

GERALD. Good night, Clive, old boy.

CLIVE. Good night.

GERTRUDE. (*Heard off.*) Clive!

CLIVE. Blast!! (*Exits* R. C., *closes door.*)

(GERALD *is staring straight in front.*)

(RHODA *exits into bedroom* L.)

SLOW CURTAIN.

(SECOND CURTAIN: GERALD *is seen with his pyjama coat; he picks up a pair of flannel trousers and sits on the sofa, preparatory to turning in.*)

CURTAIN.

ACT II

SCENE: *The hall next morning. Bright sunshine is seen through the open doorway. The hall has been cleared and the portmanteau and unpacking have disappeared.*

(GERALD *and* CLIVE *in fresh, clean attire are talking things over.* CLIVE *at door* R. C., GERALD *on settee* L. *up stage.*)

GERALD. So that's the whole story of why she came here.

CLIVE. 'M.

GERALD. What do you think of it?

CLIVE. (*With a grimace.*) I believe it, of course. (*Cross to above table.*)

GERALD. But you don't think anyone else would?

CLIVE. Oh, I don't know. The marines *might.*

GERALD. I know it sounds unlikely. I told her so last night.

CLIVE. It sounds a great deal worse this morning. (*Crosses to above table.*)

GERALD. Why? I haven't seen her since last night.

CLIVE. I quite believe that too. But I wouldn't press that even on a marine.

Gerald. You don't think Clara would accuse me?

Clive. (*Shrugs, crosses behind to table* L. C.) I don't know. You see, you've been married such a short time.

Gerald. Yes. (*Smiling.*) That's an advantage.

Clive. Is it?

Gerald. (*His face falling.*) Isn't it?

Clive. Well, you can't have broken her in much in six weeks. (*Sits on table,* L. *corner up stage.*)

Gerald. Oh no, old boy. I'm sure she'll trust me.

Clive. Oh, good. I hope so, I'm sure.

Gerald. I'm certain she will. Our first night apart. (*Rising, cross* D. L.) Good Lord!

Clive. Well, that's all right then. You know her best.

Gerald. Yes. Oh, Clara won't suspect me for a moment.

Clive. Fine. There you are, then.

Gerald. I mean, of course, if she doesn't hear anything about it.

Clive. Oh, I thought you meant you'd tell her.

Gerald. Tell her? Oh, why? If we get this girl away there'll be nothing to tell. (*Cross* R. C.)

Clive. If Gertrude finds out—Clara will be told all right.

Gerald. She'll be told all wrong. If there's a chance of that I must tell Clara first.

Clive. Oh yes, old boy, I should tell her in any case. You know—airily, as if you had nothing on your conscience—I should say (*acting*) Ha!

rather a funny thing happened the other night. A little girl drifted in here—pretty little thing she was—no, perhaps you hadn't better say that—driven from home.

Gerald. You think that sounds as if you've nothing on your conscience?

Clive. Well, it's difficult for me to say what a married man's conscience is like—me being single mine's rather elastic. (*Crosses* R. *to front of table.*)

Gerald. Much better get the girl some clothes and take her away.

Clive. Yes. You're quite right. (*An afterthought.*) What's the time?

Gerald. (*Looking at his watch.*) Oh, about a quarter-past.

Clive. A quarter-past eight?

Gerald. Yes.

Clive. (*Jumping up.*) Well, what about eight-thirty?

Gerald. What?

Clive. The daily woman, you fool.

Gerald. Good Lord, yes. Eight-thirty. Earlier than that she cannot be. (*Looks over at kitchen and crosses* R. *to* Clive.) What shall we do? She's got the back door key.

Clive. Stop her getting to the back door, that's all.

Gerald. What—you mean go and meet her?

Clive. Yes, and tell her not to come.

Gerald. (*Crossing to door* R. C.) You come *with* me. You can tackle her better than I can.

Clive. All right. You go to one gate, I'll go

to the other. You never know which way she's coming; these fat women live in all directions.

(*They exit* R. C. CLIVE *goes off* R. GERALD *is seen going off* L., *leaving door open.*)

(RHODA *comes out of bedroom* L. *and looks out of the window* C. *of balcony; she stretches her arms as she looks out.*)

(*Then the kitchen door is opened and in comes* MRS. LEVERETT. *Surprised to see the front door open, she crosses towards it and looks out. She has already removed her hat and left it in the kitchen. She stands beneath the canopy of the jutting landing. By standing where she is* MRS. LEVERETT *can see without being seen. Her expression becomes one of furious amazement as she hears* RHODA *call.*)

RHODA. (*Comes to front of balcony and looks down into hall—calling softly.*) Mr. Popkiss! Mr. Popkiss!

(*No reply.* RHODA *turns and goes back into the bedroom, again closing the door.* MRS. LEVERETT *comes forth from her hiding-place as though in a sort of indignant trance. Then she rouses herself to action; hurries into the kitchen; hurries out again, putting on her hat as she does so and, after taking another look at the bedroom door, goes quickly away through the kitchen. Closes door.*)

(*Voices are heard outside* R. C. *The first person who appears is* TWINE, *who is in plus fours. He is speaking over his shoulder as he enters* R. C. *from* R.)

TWINE. Well, now that I am here—(*anxiously*) come inside, please. (*Cross to* R. *of table.*)

CLIVE. (*Following.*) Why? (*Cross door* R. C.)

TWINE. I don't want to be seen.

CLIVE. Oh, I shouldn't worry. You look fairly all right.

TWINE. No, but I told Gertrude I'd go to the golf club. She asked where you were. I said I didn't know.

CLIVE. I see. And you came over here because of your last night swear?

TWINE. I felt it my duty to come here.

CLIVE. And I don't believe you'd have come at all, if I hadn't caught you dithering at the gate.

TWINE. You don't seem to realise I told Gertrude I was going straight up to the golf club. (*Turning away.*) I've told her a *lie.*

CLIVE. Oh, that's nothing. You'll do better than that.

TWINE. Oh, but, Clave——

CLIVE. What?

TWINE. (*With emotion.*) What is all this terrible affair? It must be *stopped.* (*Close to* CLIVE's *face.*)

CLIVE. Quite right, old boy; we'll stop it between us. All boys together.

TWINE. No, no; I won't be mixed up in it. I've already *lied* to Gertrude. I'm feeling very uncomfortable.

CLIVE. What, already? You *wait.*

(GERALD *returns breathlessly from rnnning past windows. Enters* R. C., *crosses to* L., *looks in kitchen.*)

GERALD. I've looked right down the road—there's no sign of that daily woman.

CLIVE	TWINE
R.	R. C.

CLIVE. Well, if she comes, we'll get rid of her somehow. I was just telling Harold—now *he's* here to help us, we'll get on better.

GERALD. (*Crossing to* R. *of table, taking* TWINE'S *hand.*) Indeed, yes. Thank you, Harold.

TWINE. Oh——

CLIVE	TWINE	GERALD
R.	R. C.	(*Front of table.*)

CLIVE. No, no—stop that!

GERALD. Yes—from the start, Harold, that "oh" business is out.

TWINE. I've lied to my wife.

GERALD. You have? Stout fellow! A very good beginning.

TWINE. Oh, don't, please! This is not the time for funning.

CLIVE. There you are. The very first comment he makes. Sound common sense. (*Slapping* TWINE *on the back.*)

GERALD. Yes. Bravo, Harold!

CLIVE. Now, first of all, you've got to believe, Harold, that that girl is a pure, nice, good, innocent little child.

GERALD. Absolutely. I know it's hard for you to believe, Harold, because a man like you—a man of the world, who's knocked about with all sorts of wild women——

Clive. Yes, of course—when a man like this sees a girl in your house, naturally he leaps to conclusions.

Gerald. Leaps—why, he bounds!

Clive. Yes, the old scoundrel—he's been knee-deep in daisies many a time.

Twine. Oh——

Clive. Ah!

Gerald. Another "oh" and we shall have to swear you about it.

Twine. The girl's got a very queer reputation, anyhow.

Gerald. Yes, and who queered it?

Clive. Now, look here, Twine. Experience may have made you a cynic about women. (*Crosses down* R.) Possibly you may have been stung once too often. (*Coming back* R. C.) But, believe me, old boy, there can still be such a thing as a good girl.

Gerald. Yes, Harold. Even in the same town as you.

Twine. Then why should she be here—at night, in——

Clive. In what?

Twine. (*Hesitating.*) Well, wearing those things——

Gerald. She was run out.

Twine. What?

Clive. She had trouble at home. You know what trouble at home is, don't you?

Twine. Yes.

Clive. Yes, none better.

Gerald. You'd better see her for yourself and judge. (*Crosses* L. C.)

Twine. Why, good *heavens*, is she *still* here?

Gerald. Yes, of course she is—up in that bedroom. I'll introduce you. (*Turns to go upstairs* L.)

Twine. (*Cross in front of table to* L. C.) No, no, no. I'm going to golf. (*Edging towards* R. C. *door*.)

Clive *and* Gerald. (*Who pause incredulously on stairs*.) Golf!

Twine. Yes. I'd rather go to golf.

Clive. You'd rather golf than see this girl?

Twine. Much.

Gerald. You'd rather golf *much*? (*At top of stairs* L.)

Twine. Yes. Not only that, I told Gertrude. Besides, I've got a match.

Clive. But dash it, man, *noblesse oblige*.

Gerald. Yes, and *honi soit*—you stay there. (*Goes to bedroom door up* L. *and knocks*.)

Rhoda. (*From inside bedroom*.) Come in.

Gerald. No, you come out.

(Rhoda *appears*.)

Rhoda. Good morning.

Gerald. Good morning.

Rhoda. (*To* Clive.) Good morning.

Clive. (*Heartily*.) Good morning.

(Gerald *goes down two or three stairs* L. *Introduction*.)

Gerald. Here we are. Mr. Harold Twine—Miss Rhoda Something.

Rhoda. Good morning. Rhoda Marley, my name is.

Clive. (*To* Twine.) Go on—How do you do?

Twine. (*Unable to resist*.) How do you do?

CLIVE. Good! Well, now that you've how do you done, just look at that girl.

GERALD. (*Beaming at* RHODA.) Yes.

CLIVE. I mean, can you, Harold—can you possibly suspect?

TWINE. (*Feebly.*) N-n-no.

GERALD. No. Come on, heartily, Harold. *No.*

CLIVE. Perish the thought.

TWINE. Yes, certainly.

CLIVE. Go on then. Let's hear it.

TWINE. Perish the thought.

(CLIVE *cross* R.)

(GERALD *brings* RHODA *downstairs* L. *to* L. C.)

GERALD. And you admit that Gertrude was and is wrong in saying things about her?

TWINE. I don't know. (*Cross* L. C.)

GERALD. You *do* know, Harold.

TWINE. Oh dear, well—yes.

GERALD. So now it is your duty to make amends.

CLIVE. That's right. And to do what we tell you to help Miss Marley.

TWINE. I can't make any promise, but I'll tell you what I'll do. I'll tell Gertrude——

GERALD. What!

CLIVE. You blithering idiot!

TWINE. No, now Clave. (*To* CLIVE.) Gerald, I'll tell Gertrude I think she's made a mistake.

RHODA. (*Quickly—as* CLIVE *and* GERALD *protest.*) Please, Mr. Twine!

TWINE. What?

RHODA. I'd rather you didn't tell Mrs. Twine I'm here.

Clive. Of course he won't. Don't you worry.

Twine. (*Obstinately.*) Then I'll take no part in it at all. And in any case I've got to go to golf now. (*Turns up* r.)

(Gerald *crosses back to table to* Twine *as he attempts to go; pushes him towards* l. *and goes to door.* Twine *crosses* r. *to* Clive *as he speaks line* "I've arranged to play with Admiral Juddy." Gerald *then comes down* l. *of* Twine.)

Gerald. Harold, if this is your attitude, you'll see the inside of no bunker to-day.

Twine. But I must. I've arranged to play with Admiral Juddy.

Gerald. (*Crosses down* l. *of* Twine.) But not yet.

Twine. Yes, before nine. Because the course gets so congested at this time of year.

Clive. Well, you can't; that's all.

Twine. (*In a panic.*) Oh, but I must. You don't know Admiral Juddy.

Clive. No, and I don't want to.

(*All move down stage a little.*)

Twine. He's been years in China and he flies into rages and uses terrible expressions.

Gerald. That won't matter. You won't be there to hear them.

Rhoda. Oh please, Mr. Popkiss.

Gerald. Yes?

Clive. Yes? (*They both turn to her, softening quickly.*)

Rhoda. I'm sure Mr. Twine won't do or say

anything to hurt me if I ask him nicely. Can't he go to his golf?

TWINE. Thank you. I won't say a word about you to anyone.

GERALD. And if you can help, you will?

TWINE. Yes. Willingly.

RHODA. (*Smiling sweetly at* TWINE.) That's right.

(*Noise of door latch in kitchen* D. L.)

GERALD. (*Crosses down* L. *front of table, listening, then speaking in a hoarse whisper.*) Look out! Listen! (*At noise in kitchen—*)

TWINE O   RHODA O

CLIVE O   GERALD O

(*Then—*)

RHODA O

CLIVE O

GERALD O

TWINE O

THE OTHERS. (*Turning.*) What?

GERALD. (*As before.*) The back door. (*Crosses* L. C.). It's the d.w.

CLIVE. (*Crosses to front of table* C.) Damn it, she's come after all.

GERALD. What shall we do?

CLIVE. (*To* RHODA *and* GERALD.) You go up

in that room. (*Indicates bedroom on* L. *of balcony.*)

TWINE. (R. C. *to* CLIVE.) Who is it ?

CLIVE. The daily woman.

TWINE. (*Turning towards front door.*) Oh !

(CLIVE *catches at his arm as he attempts to go. The subsequent scene is played in quick, subdued manner.*)

CLIVE. Don't go now, you fool. She may see you and tell Gertrude. Then Gertrude will know that you've lied to her.

TWINE. Oh, my gracious !

CLIVE. You come up to that bedroom, too.

(GERALD *crosses to stairs and goes up.* RHODA *follows.* TWINE *is following behind, being hustled by* CLIVE.)

TWINE. (*Very scared.*) What, to the bedroom ? No——

CLIVE. Yes. Shut up ! (*Giving* TWINE *a lift with his knee.*) Now up you go, quick !

(RHODA *exits into bedroom.*)

TWINE. Oh !

CLIVE. Go in there. (*He turns.*)

(CLIVE *and* GERALD *shove* TWINE *into bedroom after* RHODA.)

(*Turns to* GERALD.) Gerald, you wait for her at the top of the stairs, and when you hear her coming upstairs, stand in the doorway and sack her.

GERALD. Good ! You go in, old boy.

(CLIVE *exits into bedroom.*)

TWINE. (*Reappearing in doorway.*) Look here, I say——

(*They bear him forcibly inside and close the bedroom door.*)

(*After a moment* MRS. LEVERETT *comes very stealthily into the hall. She looks about her.* GERTRUDE *follows into the hall close on her heels.*)

MRS. LEVERETT. (L. C., *with her head thrown back. Whispering hoarsely.*) If she's still here she's in the bedroom.

(*They both look up at bedroom* L.)

And also he too has gone back in there himself as well, what's more.

GERTRUDE. (L. C., *whispering back.*) It seems incredible. You honestly promise me you saw her yourself with your own eyes ?

MRS. LEVERETT. Yes, by the Testament I saw her with me hand on me heart.

GERTRUDE. (*To herself, pensively.*) H'm. Six weeks. Well, I shall know what to do if it's true. I shall go straight away to Bath and get his wife.

MRS. LEVERETT. She ought to be told.

GERTRUDE. She will be told. She'll not only be told, she'll be brought here and shown.

MRS. LEVERETT. When will you go for her, madam?

GERTRUDE. At once, if it's true.

MRS. LEVERETT. Oh, it's true enough.

GERTRUDE. (*Looking up* L.) You'd better go up and knock and see what happens.

Mrs. Leverett. (*Crosses to foot of stairs* L.) Yes.

Gertrude. Don't appear to suspect anything.

Mrs. Leverett. No. (*Going upstairs.*)

Gertrude. I shall wait by the back door. (*Crosses to door* D. L.) You come out and tell me what happens.

Mrs. Leverett. Yes.

Gertrude. Very likely you'll find there's no one in the room at all.

Mrs. Leverett. (*Very certain.*) Oh! (*Goes up two or three stairs.*)

Gertrude. If so, go along there to the room I told him to sleep in and see if he's there.

Mrs. Leverett. Yes.

Gertrude. Go on then. You'd better not be wearing your hat. Give it to me.

(Mrs. Leverett *hands it to her. Goes upstairs quietly and listens outside bedroom door. Then knocks. Immediately the bedroom door flies open.* Mrs. Leverett *falls back a step or two, as* Gerald *stands in a commanding attitude in the doorway.* Gertrude *waits in a listening attitude at the foot of the stairs, just inside the kitchen door* L.)

Gerald. (*Loudly.*) What! At *this* hour?

Mrs. Leverett. I beg your pardon?

Gerald. *Not* granted.

Mrs. Leverett. Eh?

Gerald. How dare you do this? You're very late and very late.

(Gertrude *exits* D. L.)

If you can't come here at all, don't come here at the proper time.

MRS. LEVERETT. I don't understand your meaning.

GERALD. Luckily for you. You—you dare to come here like this, hours afterwards, crawling upstairs like a balloon——

MRS. LEVERETT. Balloon!

GERALD. Yes, and me with no tea and early cot hold water—shave—you know—hot pot tea and shaving—go away with you—right away——

MRS. LEVERETT. I'm not far be'ind me time. I have come here as promised. What more do you want me to do?

GERALD. There's only one thing for you to do, and that is your old friend, the quit.

(GERTRUDE *exits into kitchen* D. L.)

MRS. LEVERETT. Oh, indeed! Very well, then.

GERALD. Yes, awfully well then.

MRS. LEVERETT. You don't want me here?

GERALD. Not a bit of you.

MRS. LEVERETT. Oh, in that case——

GERALD. Yes?

MRS. LEVERETT. I say, in that case—I give you a week's notice.

GERALD. (*Taken aback.*) A week?

MRS. LEVERETT. (*Turning to go downstairs.*) Yes. A week from now.

GERALD. Oh! (*Prompted evidently from the bedroom.*) What? Wait a minute! Oh yes, I know. Here! You're going to be weighed——

MRS. LEVERETT. What?

(*Warning for door slam.*)

GERALD. Paid—you're going to be paid off now. How much?

MRS. LEVERETT. H'm—you seem in a great hurry to——

GERALD. Not a word. How much?

MRS. LEVERETT. I'll take a pound——

GERALD. (*Over his shoulder.*) She'll take a pound. (*Correcting the impression that he was addressing anyone else by grinning at* MRS. LEVERETT, *then correcting himself for grinning.*) You'll take a pound.

(GERALD *turns to go into bedroom.* MRS. LEVERETT *attempts to go into bedroom, but* GERALD *stops her.*)

Stay there!

(*She takes two steps back upstairs; he goes in and shuts door.* MRS. LEVERETT *nods to herself triumphantly and moves to bedroom door again.*)

(*He reappears. Nearly bumping her with door.*)

Take this and go. (*Hands her a pound note.*)

MRS. LEVERETT. I did not like the looks of you from the start.

GERALD. And I don't like the look of you at the finish.

MRS. LEVERETT. (*Coming downstairs.*) Very good then. I may say I'd 'ave *given* this *not* to work here.

GERALD. Why didn't you say that before?

(*She goes out indignantly and shuts door* D. L.)
(*Short pause before door slam off* L.)
(*He runs down the stairs and listens. A door is heard to slam off* L. *He crosses to* C. *and calls to* CLIVE *and* TWINE *up* L.)

(*Crosses* D. L. *to* C.) Come on; it's all right. She's gone.

(CLIVE *comes downstairs, followed by* RHODA *and* TWINE.)

CLIVE. I don't think you did that very well.
GERALD. Well, she's gone anyhow.
TWINE. Yes, and I must go now, please. (*Crosses to* L. C.)
GERALD. (*Detaining him.*) s it all clear for Harold now?
CLIVE. Yes, let him go.
TWINE. I must, please. Admiral Juddy——
CLIVE. All right—go.
TWINE. Yes. (*Starting up* L. C.)

(*All up stage.*)

GERALD	TWINE	CLIVE	RHODA
R. C.	L. C.	L. C.	L.

Oh—well, all right. (*Goes towards door* R. C.)
GERALD. Stay there a moment—I'll see if it's all clear.

(*He opens the door.* GERTRUDE *is standing on the threshold.*)

Not to-day, thank you. (*Closes door again and turns breathlessly.*) Gertrude!

Twine. (*Letting himself go, below his breath.*) My God !

(*Stands by door* R. C. Clive *steers* Rhoda *across* R. *and opens door* D. R., *pushing her in ; he then bundles* Twine *in, closes door* D. R.)

Gerald. (*Opening door* R. C.) Gertrude !—I beg your pardon, I thought it was the laundry.

Gertrude. (*Entering* R. C., *leaving door open—quite amiably.*) I thought you didn't see who it was. Oh, good morning, Clive.

Clive. Good morning, Gertrude.

Gertrude. You must have found your way over here very early this morning.

Clive. Yes, I thought poor old Gerald might want help.

Gerald. Yes. (*Above table.*)

Gertrude. Why, hasn't Mrs. Leverett arrived ? (*Crosses* L. *of table.*)

Gerald. Oh, most.

Gertrude. What ?

Gerald. Most attractive—er—attentive.

Gertrude. And the room I chose for you was quite comfortable ?

Gerald. Oh, more.

Gertrude. You slept well ?

Gerald. More—er—most—er—quite.

Gertrude. Oh !

(Clive, *with a frown at* Gerald, *strolls up near study door.*)

Well (*crosses to* L. *of table* C.), my reason for coming over so early was that I've had a card from Clara.

GERALD. Oh, Clara! Yes, I remember. Oh yes, my wife—I mean—yes? Well, have you brought the postcard?

GERTRUDE. No, I left it at home. Apparently, mother is still very seedy.

GERALD. Really. That's very sad—and—terribly awful.

GERTRUDE. So I'm afraid it will be quite out of the question for Clara to come on here to-day.

(GERALD *and* CLIVE *exchange glances.*)

GERALD. Oh!

GERTRUDE. She asked me to come and break it to you.

GERALD. Yes. (*Assumes very saddened expression.*)

GERTRUDE. And to make matters worse (*casually*), I'm afraid I've arranged to be away all day myself.

CLIVE. What a pity!

(GERTRUDE, *tidying cushions on settee* L., *takes a sly look at bedroom door on balcony* L.)

GERALD. Oh! (*Assumes even more sadness.*)

(CLIVE *signals to him not to overdo it.*)

GERTRUDE. So you two must keep each other company and get on as best you can.

GERALD. (*Looking at* CLIVE.) We'll do that.

GERTRUDE. Harold will be free later.

GERALD. Yes; he's gone up to the golf club.

(CLIVE *digs* GERALD *with his knee.* GERALD'S *knees give way through the shock, and he has to hold on to the corner of the table.* GERTRUDE *is looking on, so he turns it off by doing a few gymnastics; stand balancing on the same place.*)

Gertrude. Why, have you seen him then?

Gerald. Yes. (Clive *digs him.*) No, he—he told me last night he was going early to play much golf—golf much—this morning—all the morning—early this morning.

Gertrude. I see. And what will you do with yourselves?

Gerald. Yes.

Gertrude. Just take it easy. I should.

Clive. I shall knit.

Gertrude. You've got a nice long time in front of you, with nothing to worry about. Then I'll say good-bye (*crosses to door* R. C.) till this evening.

Gerald. Thank you very much.

Gertrude. What?

Gerald. I beg your pardon.

(Gertrude *goes off* R. C. *to* L.)

(Twine *enters cautiously from study, and he,* Clive *and* Gerald *exchange confidential grimaces.*)

Twine. Has she gone?

Clive. Yes.

Gerald. Yes.

(Juddy *is heard off* L. *talking to* Gertrude.)

Juddy. (*Off* L.) Day ter yah.

Gertrude. (*Off* L.) Good morning, Admiral Juddy.

(Clive, Gerald, *and* Twine *exclaim* "Juddy!" Clive *and* Gerald *bundle* Twine *back into the study.* Clive *closes the door as* Juddy *appears at door* R. C. *with* Gertrude.)

GERTRUDE. (*At door* R. C.) Harold has gone on a long time.

(ADMIRAL JUDDY, *a fierce and weather-beaten veteran with heavy eyebrows, pounds on to the scene. He is heated and annoyed. He has a habit of relieving his feelings in Chinese oaths below his breath.*)

JUDDY. He has not.

GERTRUDE. What?

JUDDY. Not! (*Crosses to* L. *of table, glares at* GERALD *and curses in Chinese below his breath.*)

(GERALD *and* CLIVE *stand close together* R.)

GERTRUDE. But he left the house over half an hour ago.

CLIVE. I saw him go myself.

(CLIVE *and* GERALD *are* R., GERTRUDE R. C., JUDDY L. C.)

JUDDY. I didn't say he didn't leave the house. I said he didn't go to the b— to the b— to the golf club.

(*He has a mannerism in the form of a little bob which he does here and repeats later.* GERALD *and* CLIVE *stand arm in arm* R. *and imitate the bobbing of* JUDDY.)

GERALD. (*To* CLIVE.) It's all right. Stand firm. Hearts of oak.

GERTRUDE. Where do you suppose he went?

JUDDY. I called at your house to see if he'd gone, and the maid told me she'd seen him coming over here.

GERTRUDE. (*Incredulously.*) Over *here*?

JUDDY. Yes, madam, over here.

GERALD. (*To* CLIVE). Yo ho, the anchor's weighed !

GERTRUDE. He didn't come here, did he? (*To* CLIVE.)

GERALD. Not in the least.

JUDDY. Well, she said he had. Said he's probably come to see you. (*To* GERALD.) You're the tenant here, aren't you—his cousin or something?

GERALD. Jack's the boy.

GERTRUDE. He's waiting for you on the links. (*Going* R. C.) I'm going back now. I'll speak to the maid.

JUDDY. Well, I hope you'll punish her. I'm sick of these servants—gossiping and messing about instead of doing their work.

GERTRUDE. I *know* Harold was going straight to the club ; because he *told* me so. So there. (*To* GERALD.) Well, till this evening, Gerald.

GERALD. Till—till——

(GERTRUDE *exits* R. C.)

CLIVE. (*Crosses to* R. *of table. To* JUDDY.) Well, sir, look here. I think the best thing will be for you to go to the golf club as quickly as possible——

JUDDY. I'm damned if I'm going to take orders from you, sir. (*Bobbing business.*)

(GERALD *crosses* R. C. *to* CLIVE.)

CLIVE. (*Imitating business.*) No, please don't misunderstand. I was going to suggest running you up there in my cousin's car.

JUDDY. Oh, I see.

(GERALD *protests.*)

CLIVE. (*To* GERALD.) All right. We must get rid of the old blighter.

JUDDY. That's a different matter.

CLIVE. Good, then that's a bet. I'll get the car.

JUDDY. Thank yah.

(CLIVE *ignores him.*)

GERALD. (*To* CLIVE.) Clive, he said "Thank yah."

(CLIVE *exits off* R. C. *hurriedly.*)

(JUDDY *approaches* GERALD, *who flinches again.*)

JUDDY. Now, sir, this fellow Twine—(*crosses to* GERALD R. C.)—he's an infernal nuisance.

GERALD. Yes. Oh! he's very troublesome.

JUDDY. Timid little ass. (*His manner is very fierce.*)

(GERALD *changes his ground again.*)

GERALD. (*As he moves away.*) Yes. I hate that sort of thing.

JUDDY. (*Going to him again.*) He's the same at everything. Golf—bridge—now, bridge. Yesterday at the club he was my partner. I dealt and called a brace of shovels. No—no—no. Right. Two shovels it was. This feller here led something—I don't know—a small sparkler. Twine, if you please, lays down a hand stiff with blood-thumpers.

GERALD. Not really? Stiff?

JUDDY. Yes, stiff. And never a murmur! Don't you understand—he ought to have called!

GERALD. Called! He ought to have screamed!

JUDDY. Of course. There it was, I lost six tricks. He hadn't a trump in his hand—where were they?

GERALD. Up his sleeve.

JUDDY. Don't you play this game?

(CLIVE *in car starts from off* R. *and pulls up outside door* R. C.)

(JUDDY *turns away up stage disgusted, swearing in Chinese.*)

P'twee! Pong choo! (*To* GERALD.) Day to yer. Blast yeh!

CLIVE. (*Stopping at window in car.*) Come on, sir. The car's alongside.

JUDDY. Right away then. Don't keep me hanging about all day, *etc. etc.*

(*Exit, raging, door up* R.)

(JUDDY *gets in car talking volubly, and while he is still standing the car starts, throwing him into seat, his hat flying off into the roadway as the car disappears off* L.)

(GERALD *closes door* R. C. *and goes to study* D. R., *opens the door and brings* RHODA *on by the hand; she crosses* L. C.)

GERALD. (*Looking into study.*) Twine, where are you? Come out from under that arm-chair. Old Jetty's gone.

(*Enter* TWINE D. R., *closes door.* GERALD *crosses* C. *in front of table.* TWINE R. C.)

RHODA. (*Cross* C.) I've told Mr. Twine all about it.

GERALD. (*To* RHODA.) Right! (*Then to* TWINE.) Now the first thing to do is for one of us to go to her house and get her clothes from Putz.

TWINE. Yes, but who?

GERALD. One of us. I'd like to go myself, only if I go I shall have to leave you alone with Rhoda. (TWINE *smiles.*) But of course Gertrude would very likely come back.

TWINE. Oh! (*Face falls.*)

GERALD. So that's agreed; he'll get them all right. (*To* RHODA.) He's a man of great strength of character; he carries a lot of weight.

TWINE. (*Modestly.*) Oh no.

GERALD. Oh, you're a member of the Urban District Council.

TWINE. Yes.

GERALD. And—(*to* RHODA)—he's President of the Girls' Friendly Society.

TWINE. No, not *this* year.

GERALD. Oh! Too friendly *last* year. (*Taking* TWINE *to door* R. C.) Well, all you have to do is to see Putz, get clothes—come back.

TWINE. I'd rather not.

GERALD. You'll find Putz an awfully nice chap.

TWINE. Shall I?

(GERALD *opens door* R. C.)

GERALD. Oh, awful.

(*Exit* TWINE R. C.)

(GERALD *closes door after him.*)

RHODA. I expect you want to get me out of the way soon, don't you?

GERALD. Yes. There's no great hurry. Mrs. Twine's gone away for the day. (*To settee* L.; *she sits up stage.*)

(GERALD *sits on table facing her.*)

RHODA. Well, I suppose—I don't know much about things, and I didn't realise at the time. But when I woke up here this morning, I thought it over and I saw what—what the world might think—isn't that the expression?

GERALD. (*Getting closer, crosses to settee, leans over back.*) Don't worry about the silly old world. There's plenty of other places besides that.

RHODA. I suppose it's because human nature is so cruel that people always think the worst.

GERALD. No, I think it's that the worst is the most likely.

RHODA. Whatever anybody thinks, you've been tremendously kind to me.

(*Warning for Dog.*)

GERALD. Yes, haven't I? No, I mustn't say that. (*About to smooth her hair, but stops.*)

RHODA. I say it anyhow; you've been wonderful.

(*He holds her hand for a moment and then lets it fall, then moves down stage behind settee.*)

RHODA. (*In a more practical voice.*) Well, the thing now is to get away.

GERALD. Yes. My cousin's going to take you in the car. Where do you want to go?

RHODA. I've got friends in London. (*Moves down to* GERALD *on settee.*)

GERALD. (*Crosses to top of settee.*) Oh! Then you'd better go to London.

RHODA. The station will do.

GERALD. Well, we'll see. First of all, what about some breakfast?

RHODA. Is there any?

GERALD. Well, tea. There's surely tea.

RHODA. Shall I skirmish for tea?

GERALD. Right you are.

(*Dog growl.*)

(TWINE *entering at door* R. C. *breathlessly.*)

TWINE. Saved!

GERALD. (*Looking round at front door, then at* RHODA.) Here's another skirmish.

(*He opens front door.* CONRAD *is heard in the distance.* TWINE, *very heated and breathless, appears at front door.*)

You've been very quick, Harold.

TWINE. Yes, I—(*out of breath*) I had to be—oh, my goodness——

GERALD. Don't stand there sizzling. Tell me what happened. (*Brings chair down to table.*)

RHODA. Did you see my step-father?

TWINE. (*Coming in, mopping his brow*). I—I *saw* him.

GERALD. Did you go to the house?

TWINE. I didn't get as far as the house.

GERALD. Why not? Did you get stung by a butterfly or something?

TWINE. No, there was a dog.

RHODA. Oh! Was the dog *loose*?

TWINE. Yes, very.

GERALD. But a dog—good Lord! What's a dog? Do you think I'm afraid of a dog?

TWINE. *You* may not be. (*Cross* D. R.)

GERALD. I should think not. (*Crosses to door* R. C., *opens it.*) *You* go back.

RHODA. Wait a moment. You say you saw my step-father?

TWINE. Yes, he came to the gate and—er—leant——

GERALD. Lent what?

TWINE. Over.

RHODA. Did he seem more polite?

TWINE. No, he didn't.

RHODA. Oh! (*Very perturbed.*)

GERALD. What did he say?

TWINE. I told him what I wanted. He said something I didn't understand. Then he said something to the dog. I didn't understand that either.

GERALD. But the dog did.

TWINE. Yes. (*Quickly.*) It appeared to. (*Looks round at door* R. C. *furtively.*)

GERALD. (*To* RHODA.) You'll be here for breakfast.

(TWINE *sits* R. *of table.*)

RHODA. Yes. Skirmish for tea.

(*She exits* D. L.)

GERALD. (*Coming and sitting down beside* TWINE *on sofa.*) Well, I'm very glad you went over.

TWINE. Glad? (*Rising*—GERALD *puts him down.*)

GERALD. Yes. Now you can see the kind of man we're up against.

TWINE. Yes.

GERALD. I've got a little scheme. The situation may yet be saved.

TWINE. By me? (*Trying to rise again.*)

GERALD. (*Putting him down.*) Yes. Don't keep popping up and down like that, old boy. You're already hot. Now this is my great idea. This girl must get some attire.

TWINE. It's all very well to say that——

GERALD. Now don't interrupt. Gertrude has gone out for the day.

TWINE. Gertrude? No.

(TWINE *is fidgeting with his trousers.*)

GERALD. Yes. She said so herself. Don't fiddle about with your knickers, old boy. We must concentrate. As I say, this girl must have something to wear.

(TWINE, *inquiring look.*)

And Gertrude has gone out for the day.

TWINE. Well?

(GERALD *taps his knee and speaks emphatically.*)

GERALD. As I say, the girl must have some female garments—well, Gertrude has plenty. And she has gone out for the day.

(TWINE *slowly turns a horrified expression of inquiry towards* GERALD. *The latter pulls out a cigarette case.*)

Have a cigarette, old boy?

TWINE. No, thanks. D'you mean—?

GERALD. Yes, by Jove! you're a marvel. I don't know anyone who would have seen it so quickly.

TWINE. (*Rising.*) You don't really seriously

suggest that I should go and get some clothes of Gertrude's?

Gerald. (*Rising.*) Well, old boy, you had your chance of getting Rhoda's own clothes from Putz. You come back sizzling with your stocking half mast and say we can't get them. Well, we must get some.

(Twine *fiddles about.*)

Keep still—do. I've told you that before. Have you got woollies on? Now listen—if you get some things of Gertrude's——

Twine. *That* I positively will not do.

Gerald. (*Incredulously.*) You won't get them?

Twine. Absolutely no.

Gerald. You—in fact—you don't agree with my idea?

Twine. No. Certainly not.

Gerald. No. Well, well—it's a pity, but there you are. The best of friends must differ.

(Clive *enters* R. C. *quietly and stands just inside door.*)

Twine. I abso——

Gerald. Now, old boy. No need to be pugnacious about it. I'm perfectly sure that I'm right, but you don't hear *me* saying I abso——

Twine. Nothing will induce me.

(Clive *stands inside doorway* R. C.)

Gerald. Quite. Quite.

(Gerald *looks at* Clive.)

And mark you, you may be justified. I want to be quite fair. I say it's a good idea, you say no.

Of course what one really wants in these cases is a third party—as referee.

TWINE. Nobody would persuade me.

GERALD. Now, there you lose sympathy. For my part I'd agree to abide by a third party's decision. Of course we must find somebody entirely disinterested—you agree to that (*taking it for granted*)—yes. (*Look at* CLIVE.) Now, who can we find? You don't know anyone, I suppose?

(TWINE *stares vacantly.*)

TWINE. No.

GERALD. Old boy, I've got it.

TWINE. What?

GERALD. Clive shall decide.

TWINE. *No.* (*Nervously.*)

GERALD. Oh, who better! He's neutral. We'll put it to him.

TWINE. Oh!

GERALD. Now personally I think you'll win.

(TWINE *smiles broadly.* CLIVE *slams door* R.)

CLIVE. Hallo, boys!

GERALD. Hallo, Clive!

CLIVE. What's up?

GERALD. Harold and I are just holding what might be called an extraordinary general meeting.

CLIVE. Oh? (*Surprised.*)

GERALD. We're at a deadlock about a certain proposition and need an arbitrator, and we thought of you.

CLIVE. Thank you very much, Harold—that's nice of you. What's the snag?

GERALD. This. (*Pacifying* TWINE.) No, I'll

put it fairly. We can't get a rig-out from Putz. But a rig-out for this girl we must have.

Clive. There can't be any dispute about that.

Gerald. No. Oh no. But Gertrude having gone for the day——

Clive. Yes, I saw her go off in her car——

Gerald. Yes, I was telling Harold about that. Well, one of us says "Get a rig-out from Gertrude's wardrobe." The other says "No." That's all.

Clive. Oh, don't be a blithering idiot.

Gerald. You think I'm wrong?

Clive. Wrong? Of course you're wrong.

(Twine *is very pleased.*)

Gerald. (*To* Twine.) It's all right—you've won.

Clive. Here's a heaven-sent inspiration, and you turn it down. (*To* Twine.) Congratulations, Harold.

(Gerald *crosses to settee, sits* L.)

Twine. I beg your pardon?

Clive. I think it's a fine idea of yours. I unhesitatingly vote for it.

Twine. But I'm against it.

Clive. Against it?

Gerald. Yes, old boy, I don't want to boast, but I'm the one who said "Do it."

Clive. It doesn't make any difference. My decision stands. It's the best idea of the whole morning, and, besides, Gertrude has got some very nice things.

Gerald. Well, then, I think—the sooner the better. What?

Twine. (*Jumping up.*) Listen, you fellows——

Clive. No. *You* listen for a change. You've done nothing but yap, yap, yap all the morning. Just think what we've done for you. We hid you from Gertrude. We saved you when that Admiral came in here, breathing fire from his nostrils.

(Clive *and* Gerald *exchange looks.*)

Twine. Yes, I dare say. Thanks.

Clive. We're not asking for gratitude. But something has got to be done quickly—poor old Gerald may get into trouble.

Gerald. Yes. That's the most important point.

Clive. And we must stand by him. We're in the same camp.

Gerald. Yes. And we must have loyalty in the camp.

Clive. Yes. And if necessary enforce it.

Twine. (*Nervously.*) What?

Clive. The alternative is surrender. Make a clean breast of it all to Gertrude——

Gerald. And the Admiral——

Clive. Tell Gertrude the girl was in that study while she was in the hall——

Gerald. And you were in that study——

Clive. With the girl——

Gerald. Alone——

Clive. For a long time. *Or*—keep Gertrude from finding out——

Gerald. Ever——

Clive. By getting the girl some clothes.

(*Pause.* Twine *stands miserably.* Gerald *speaks dramatically into his ear.*)

GERALD. So clothes——

CLIVE. Or Gertrude——

CLIVE *and* GERALD. Choose!

(TWINE *only moans.* GERALD *and* CLIVE *lift* TWINE *by the arms and seat him on the table.*)

(GERALD *turns to* CLIVE *practically.*)

CLIVE. Carried.

GERALD. Now, what will she want?

CLIVE. We'd better ask Rhoda what she wants. Where is she?

(GERALD *turns to the kitchen door* D. L. TWINE *attempts to go, but* CLIVE *holds him by the arm.*)

GERALD. (*Speaking into kitchen.*) How are you getting on?

RHODA. (*Off* L.) Splendidly. I've found some tea.

GERALD. We want you here a minute.

RHODA. Yes?

(GERALD *crosses* L. RHODA *enters* L., *crosses to* L. C.)

GERALD. Mr. Twine is just going to get some clothes.

CLIVE. Some of Mrs. Twine's.

RHODA. Oh, but really——

CLIVE. Well?

RHODA. It's very kind of Mr. Twine to think of it—but I couldn't wear hers.

TWINE. No. You see?

RHODA. I mean they'd be too old for me.

GERALD. Oh, but she's got some new ones.

CLIVE. (*To* GERALD.) No, you fool. (*Crossing to* RHODA.) It's simply to have an outfit here in case you can't get your own.

RHODA. Oh, I see.

CLIVE. Yes. Now what will you want? Will you just tick off the items with Mr. Twine?

(TWINE *attempts to go*—CLIVE *holds him by the arm.*)

RHODA. Well, it's very kind of Mr. Twine——

GERALD. Never mind that. Tick off the items.

RHODA. Well, just a frock and something to go under it.

GERALD. (*Severely to* TWINE.) Do you know what goes under it?

CLIVE. All right, *I* know. I'll tell him. (*To* TWINE.) A bodice.

GERALD. (*To* TWINE.) Has Gertrude got a bodice?

TWINE. (*Resignedly.*) Oh, I suppose so.

CLIVE. You mustn't suppose.

GERALD. No—you must know. You've been married for years. Get a bodice.

TWINE. All right. A bust one.

GERALD. (*In horror.*) Certainly not—a sound one.

CLIVE. (*To* GERALD.) That's all right.

GERALD. Is it?

CLIVE. Yes. Bust. You know. Be careful what you're saying!

GERALD. Oh, sorry. Harold began it.

CLIVE. Well, then, a frock and its underneath——

RHODA. And, I suppose, some shoes and stockings——

Clive. (*To* Twine.) Only with the stockings you'll want—(*trying to be tactful*)—to arrange for them to keep up.

Rhoda. (*To* Gerald.) And possibly a hat if he can manage it.

Gerald. Oh, easily. (*To* Twine.) Manage a hat. And choose the things that Gertrude won't miss. Put 'em all in a bag.

Twine. (*With the air of one delivering an ultimatum.*) When I've done this, I've finished with you.

Gerald. Then do it quickly.

Clive. You can take Gerald's car. Go on.

Gerald. (*Turns, crosses towards* R. C.) Steady on, old boy, it's my car.

Clive. Yes, let him have the car.

Gerald. All right. (*To* Twine.) Hurry up then. Hop in the car. (*Taking* Twine's *arm and leading him to front door.*) I'll see you off.

Twine. (*Trying to shake* Gerald *off.*) Oh, let me go!

Gerald. (*Turning to* Clive *as he takes* Twine *out.*) There you are. He *wants* to go.

(Gerald *goes out with* Twine R. C.)

Rhoda. (*To* Clive.) Oh, Mr. Popkiss——

Clive. Yes?

Rhoda. Do you mind if I ask you something? I want your advice.

Clive. Do you? Come on then. (*Cross to table* C.) Sit down here and tell me all about it. (*Sitting on table.*)

(Clive R. C. Rhoda L. C.)

Rhoda. It's only—I couldn't help coming here. But isn't it my duty now to give in and go home?

CLIVE. Your duty—who to ? Me ?

RHODA. No. I meant to your cousin.

CLIVE. Oh, old Gerald—but you needn't worry any more about *him*. You're not going to stay here anyhow. You're coming with me in the car, aren't you ?

RHODA. Yes, if you—really—don't mind.

CLIVE. If *I* don't mind ! You needn't let that worry you. But you like to come with me, don't you ?

RHODA. Yes.

CLIVE. I'll take great care of you.

RHODA. I'm sure you will. I knew that directly I saw you.

CLIVE. Did you ? That's fine, because, you know, directly I saw *you* I knew something too. When you came out of that room last night on to the landing and smiled that little smile of yours—

(*She smiles.*)

yes—that's the one—do you know what I knew then ?

RHODA. No——

CLIVE. (*Seeing her embarrassment.*) Well—I—er—never mind—we've plenty of time for that. Anyhow, you're glad you're coming with me in the car, aren't you ?

RHODA. Yes, very. But I want to go to friends in London. Can you *go* all that way ?

CLIVE. Can I ? You try and think of some friends in Scotland !

(*She smiles again.*)

What a bit of luck that I'm here, isn't it? (*Taking her hand.*)

Rhoda. (*Again embarrassed.*) Yes.

(Clive, *hands bus.:* Clive *takes* Rhoda's *right hand in his left, palm to palm, and with his right hand lifts her fingers, letting them drop back.*)

Clive. I mean—of course, old Gerald would probably take you himself if I wasn't here. I say, isn't that funny? Do you see the way your fingers flop back, like a piano? He's married—and so on.

Rhoda. Yes. I'm afraid I've done quite enough to compromise him already.

Clive. Yes—I didn't mean that—but what I meant was—it would be wasted on him.

Rhoda. Oh, I see. Then—*you're not* married?

Clive. Me? No, I'm not married. Not—yet.

Rhoda. Oh. Then you're going to be?

Clive. What? Well, I—I didn't think so; but if—I—— (*Hums a few bars of a song.*)

(Gerald *enters* r. c., *comes down* r., *and* Clive *sees him.*)

Rhoda. Oh, I think the kettle's boiling.

Gerald. Oh, is it? Good! (*Makes no effort to go.*)

Rhoda. I'd better see to it. (*Goes to kitchen.*)

Clive. Yes, I'll come with you. (*Going after her.*)

Gerald. No, stay here, old boy.

Clive. Oh, but I haven't seen a kettle boil for years!

GERALD. (*Holding door* D. L.) This is no time for kettling. Quick now! What are we going to do? (*Cross* R. C.)

CLIVE. She's coming with me.

GERALD. In Gertrude's clothes? (R. C.)

CLIVE. Yes. Why not?

GERALD. This is desperate stuff.

CLIVE. I know, but every minute's delay is dangerous.

GERALD. But Gertrude's gone away.

CLIVE. Other people will see her.

GERALD. Who?

CLIVE. Tradesmen, you fool. Milkmen—gardeners—probably the vicar.

GERALD. Yes, all right, old boy. Don't be impulsive. It was I who said we must do something quickly.

CLIVE. Well, do it.

GERALD. But do you think she'll be all right in Gertrude's things?

CLIVE. Of course she will. She'd look lovely in anything.

GERALD. I don't mean that. You don't have to tell me that. I've known her a good deal longer than you have. I mean, oughtn't we to get her own if we can?

CLIVE. And let Putz know that we're trying to smuggle her away?

GERALD. What about an offensive on Putz? A combined offensive?

CLIVE. No. Cut Putz clean out of it.

(PUTZ *appears silently* R. C. *and walks slowly down* R., *unnoticed.*)

Unless, of course, we can *wangle* her things from Putz.

GERALD. Ah! By diplomacy with Putz?

CLIVE. Yes. But better ignore him completely.

GERALD. Simply don't see him at all.

CLIVE. No. Let sleeping dogs lie.

(PUTZ *is now down* R. C.)

GERALD. Quite right, old boy. *You're* right. (*Turns and sees* PUTZ, *assumes a false heartiness in his embarrassment.*) Hallo!

PUTZ. (*With challenge.*) Who shall go out from hereout in a motor? (*Pointing through window up* L.)

GERALD. He heard what we were saying.

PUTZ. Not only do I hear, I see him. Who shall go?

GERALD. Oh, you mean, who went?

PUTZ. Aller right. Who shall vent?

CLIVE. (*Crosses to* PUTZ.) You think that your step-daughter's gone. Well, allow me to tell you she's going, and you needn't think you're going to stop her. So you'd better not come and try any of your bluff on us, you damn great stiff. (*To* GERALD.) Introduce me, will you?

PUTZ. Speak. (*To* CLIVE.)

CLIVE. Well, what d'you think I'm doing—singing?

PUTZ. (*Crosses* D. R., *addressing* GERALD. *Aggressively.*) Who shall go presently already in the motor hereout? Also *that* I see and hear.

GERALD. (*To* CLIVE.) Diplomacy. Oh yes! Now look. Putty, old thing. (*Approaching* PUTZ.)

(CLIVE *backs him up.*)

Don't you worry about that car. That was just my brother-in-law—or, rather, not exactly my brother-in-law—because sisters and brothers have I none. But that man's father——

PUTZ. Speak!

GERALD. Yes; try not to say that, old boy. It's just one of those little things that irk.

PUTZ. I know of you.

(GERALD *moves back.*)

(*To* GERALD.) My howskeeper she know all of it of you. Die vife of der little man she is die enemy of Rhoda. Und she is die sister of your vife. And if your vife shall come, und Rhoda remain herein der whos, it make for you some hell of a business. *Furchterlichkeit. Sturm und Drang. (Pronounced: Fear-ster-lick-kite—Fearfulness. "Sturm und Drang"—Thunder and lightning.)*

GERALD. Speak. (*Turns to* CLIVE.)

(CLIVE *crosses to* PUTZ.)

CLIVE. (*To* PUTZ.) Now, you. Quick. One way or the other. Are you going to give us her clothes or not?

PUTZ. I give.

CLIVE. What?

PUTZ. I give. I bring heah. Und I vait. Und she put on dis clode. Und she com back mit me to der hows.

CLIVE. No damn fear.

PUTZ. (*Flaring up.*) Zo. I also have no fear already. You shall try to send her from me, und, Herr Gott! I vill make for you hot like hell.

GERALD. But you ran her out.

PUTZ. You t'ink you shall send her away also from hereout? Aller right. You shall try. Mit out die clode she cannot flee. Und I keep from her die closeys aller der time.

CLIVE. (*To* GERALD.) Oh, go on. Kick him out.

GERALD. (*To* PUTZ.) Allez—Goosen-tight!

PUTZ. You t'ink you can fight it mit me, ja?

GERALD. What? (*To* CLIVE.) Tell him to go.

CLIVE. (*Cross* R. *to* PUTZ.) Get out.

PUTZ. (*Folding his arms.*) I go ven I vish.

GERALD. What can we do to make him wish? (*Crosses behind table to* R. C.)

(TWINE *enters heatedly, carrying a bag. He has a lady's hat in his hand and shoes sticking out of his pockets.*)

TWINE. Now look here, you chaps. I've brought these things, but I've determined——

(*They signal to him violently to keep quiet.*)

CLIVE. Shut up, you idiot!

PUTZ. (*Turning on them, suddenly seizing the bag from* TWINE *with an angry roar.*) Zo! You t'ink to give her die clode. You shall not it.

(*Dialogue during struggle.*)

GERALD. Hold him, Harold.

TWINE. Don't! Don't!

CLIVE. I've got him!

(*These lines are repeated until* PUTZ *is heard at door* R. C. ("I win," *etc.*).)

(PUTZ *snatches bag from* TWINE *and moves* L. C. TWINE *catches* PUTZ *by the leg and they both fall;* GERALD *throws himself on the top, catching hold of* TWINE ; *then* CLIVE *comes round top of table to* L. PUTZ *wriggles out* L. *front with bag and crosses* L. CLIVE *intercepts* PUTZ *and tries to snatch the bag—they struggle.* PUTZ *hits* CLIVE *on the head with the bag.* CLIVE *sinks on to the settee dazed.* PUTZ *then crosses behind table to door* R. C. *and—with bag raised in his right hand—exclaims :*)

PUTZ. (*At door up* R. C.) I win—Deutschland über Alles !

QUICK CURTAIN.

(SECOND CURTAIN : GERALD *is still holding* TWINE *down* C., *but he is looking at* CLIVE, *who is just recovering from the knock on his head.* RHODA *appearing at kitchen door* D. L. *with tray of tea, etc.* CLIVE *looks at her and smiles broadly.*)

ACT III

(*Door* R. C., *closed*.)

SCENE: *The hall—about two and a half hours later.*

(*The curtain rises on angry voices.* CLIVE *discovered seated on stairs;* GERALD L. C.)

CLIVE. She didn't say it to you; she said it to me.

GERALD. Liar! That's all. Liar!

CLIVE. Are you calling me a liar?

GERALD. I said to her, "He'll help us," and she said "Thank you" to me for asking you to help.

CLIVE. You know as well as I do, I said, "I'm going to help," and she, poor little soul, burst into a smile.

GERALD. That was simply because she saw your face for the first time. I did the same.

CLIVE. Ah, wait a minute. (*Crossing round back of settee to front.*) Don't you begin on faces. The enemy's well in your country if you do.

GERALD. (*Crossing to* R. C. *front of table.*) You're jealous because I found her first.

CLIVE. (*Crossing to* L. C. *front of table.*) And you're as wild as hell because she likes me best.

GERALD. Lies and muck!

CLIVE. And I like her far better than you can.

Gerald. And I like Harold better than I like you. Also Putz, Nutts, and Conrad.

Clive. You tried to keep her a secret from me. When you knew I was coming you bunged her in the kitchen along with that humming cat.

Gerald. That's another hideous lie. But I'd rather she met the cat than you.

Clive. I saved the whole situation from the start.

Gerald. What! Who started that drivelling idea for outing that woman?

Clive. What woman?

Gerald. The daily one—Mrs. Thunderguts.

Clive. That'll do. Over the only nice thing that happens in this place you butt in and down me, or try to, you blighter.

Gerald. I butt in! I like that. I come in here and find you sitting on the table holding her poor little hand and trying to sing.

Clive. I sing a damn sight better than you do. I've heard you, thank you. Like the last bit of the bath running out.

Gerald. Anyhow, I don't want you to sing any more. I promised her decent treatment.

Clive. Yes, that's just it, and now you're sorry you promised her anything.

Gerald. Oh! The champion lie. That's yours.

Clive. I'll take it. You'd send her back to Putz if I let you.

Gerald. Clive, be careful, I warn you. Don't rouse me too much. I get like a lion.

Clive. You were a damn fine lion when Putz came in this morning.

GERALD. You made a bee-line for the door.

CLIVE. I went to the door to try to cut Putz off; and what did you do?—you sat on the floor and cut poor Harold off.

GERALD. For all the use you've been you'd better clear out.

CLIVE. I'm going to, and she's coming with me. (*Cross to* L. *of table.*) She told me herself she wanted me to take her.

GERALD. I told her to tell you so, and you know it, you dog's-body.

CLIVE. (*Crossing to* GERALD, *threateningly.*) You—you——

(RHODA *has appeared above from bedroom.*)

RHODA. (*Shocked.*) Oh!

CLIVE. (*Seeing* RHODA, *starts to sing.*)—Ukelele lady.

RHODA. If you're going to quarrel about me, I'd better go home.

GERALD. (*To* RHODA.) We were only just wondering which of us was most anxious to help you.

RHODA. You're both most anxious. That's been proved. (*Coming down* L.)

GERALD. I proved it first.

CLIVE. I'm going on proving it a long time after you are.

RHODA. Well, I think I'd better go home. (*Cross front of settee to* L. C.)

GERALD. No, no. That would be a pity.

CLIVE. Pity! You're not going back there.

RHODA. Oh, I don't want to. I only meant for his sake.

GERALD. There you are—for *my* sake.

CLIVE. It's for your sake she's willing to go, and for my sake she doesn't want to.

(RHODA *moves away* L.)

GERALD. Oh, do at least be fifty-fifty while she's here.

CLIVE. Yes, all right, old boy. Sorry!

GERALD. That's all right, old boy.

RHODA. (*Crossing to* CLIVE R. C.) Only it seems hopeless. I can't really get to London without my own things.

CLIVE. (*To* GERALD.) Are you sure there are no more of Clara's things among your luggage?

GERALD. Another pair of golf shoes and two more pairs of golf stockings—oh, and an umbrella!

(GERALD *looks away.*)

CLIVE. Oh! A string of beads and we're home. (*To* RHODA.) Anyway, couldn't you trick Putz somehow?

GERALD. Me? No, old boy, I don't think so.

CLIVE. I was talking to Rhoda.

RHODA. I wonder. Of course if I went over there dressed—I mean in any old dress——

CLIVE. Well?

RHODA. I could say "Here I am—all ready to go to London," then he might give in.

GERALD. And hand over your own things?

RHODA. Yes. I know him. When he's winning he's a devil. But if he thought I'd beaten him, he might plead.

GERALD. You hear that? Just any old frock and we could get all her things from pleading Putz.

CLIVE. Yes. There's something in this. It's worth trying.

GERALD. Yes. I said so, old boy.

CLIVE. Well, we'll set about it. (*To* RHODA.) You'd better get back to that room. (*Indicating room up* L.) There's always a chance you may be seen.

RHODA. Yes. (*Going upstairs* L.) Any kind of frock would do, and I believe I could fool him.

(CLIVE *smiles at her as she goes into room up* L. *on balcony.*)

GERALD. (*To* RHODA.) Good girl. (*To* CLIVE.) Isn't she?

CLIVE. (*With smile disappearing.*) All right. Don't start that again.

GERALD. (*With a very tolerant smile.*) Now don't start arguing.

CLIVE. What? I wasn't arguing.

GERALD. I didn't say you were. I said "don't."

CLIVE. That's the same thing as saying I was.

GERALD. Oh, is it?

CLIVE. Yes, it is it.

GERALD. Then I'm sorry.

CLIVE. That's quite all right.

GERALD. Not at all, old boy. Still, personally I don't think it is.

CLIVE. You don't think it is what?

GERALD. The same thing to say to a person "don't" as to say "you are."

CLIVE. What the hell are you talking about?

GERALD. Well, old boy, you ought to know. You began it.

CLIVE. Began what? (*Raising his voice.*)

GERALD. I said "don't," and you said——

CLIVE. Don't what?

GERALD. I forget now. Oh yes, I remember. I said "don't let's argue."

CLIVE. Well, anyhow, this frock—the shops will be open now.

GERALD. But I've told you. No shops are open to-day.

CLIVE. You went down before the shops were open, and that was why you found the shops were shut.

GERALD. I keep telling you there are no shops open in the place to-day; it's a sort of local regatta.

CLIVE. (*Crosses to settee and sits.*) I know you did.

GERALD. The man who keeps the milliner's shop is in the town band.

CLIVE. I don't care if he's in the fire brigade. Round him up.

GERALD. I can't. He's in the band on the front, shaking his exhaust out of the butt end of a cornet.

CLIVE. (*Crossing to* L. C. *above table.*) Well, there are other towns within reach—without regattas.

GERALD. I never said there weren't.

CLIVE. (*Cross to* GERALD.) No, but you never remembered there *were*.

GERALD. Well, go and find one if you're so clever.

CLIVE. I'm going to, and I'm going to take the car. (*Cross up* L., GERALD R. C.)

GERALD. There you go again. My car. (*Crosses to* L. C. *front of table.*)

CLIVE. (R. C.) Well, hell's delight, it's for your sake.

GERALD. You don't say "May I take the car ?" You say "I'm going to take the car." That's what gets my goat.

CLIVE. Anyway, I bet you I get into a shop here.

GERALD. I bet you. There ! I've been and seen. The only things you can buy are flags and beer.

CLIVE. Then why didn't you get some beer ?

GERALD. I did.

CLIVE. You *would.*

GERALD. Go on. Good-bye.

(CLIVE, *going* R. C., *turns back and goes to kitchen door.*)

CLIVE. Well, I hope you'll enjoy yourself. You'll have nice company.

GERALD. (*With a smile.*) Yes. Why are you going that way ?

(JUDDY *is seen through window* R. C.)

CLIVE. Because old Admiral Bloodhead is coming up the drive.

(*Exit* D. L. *to kitchen.*)

GERALD. Oh, curse him ! What does he want ?

(*Knock at door* R. C.)

Come in.

(JUDDY *enters as* CLIVE *goes.*)

JUDDY. Hallo, yer young devil ! (*Door* R. C.) I've heard about you. Where is she ?

GERALD. Where's who ?

Judd. That girl. Come on. I'm not one of the people who abuse that girl. I like her. Like her looks. Always have.

Gerald. Yes. I always have too.

Juddy. Well, you needn't think I'm going to let her be kicked out of the house like this.

Gerald. Oh, it's not a question of her being kicked out at all.

Juddy. It is. I'm going to make the devil of a row about it.

Gerald. But, Mr.—Captain—she's not being kicked out.

Juddy. She was kicked out by that swine, wasn't she?

Gerald. Oh, by Putz. Quite right. Yes, old boy, old salt.

Juddy. How long is she going to be here?

Gerald. Well, the trouble is she's got no clothes.

Juddy. Hasn't she? Oh! (*Cross* L.) I'd rather like to have a word with her. Where is she?

Gerald. No, I'll tell you what. Have you a wife?

Juddy. It doesn't matter if I've got fifty wives.

Gerald. I refer to the one in this port.

Juddy. Eh?

Gerald. I mean what size is she?

Juddy. Mind yer own business.

Gerald. I was only thinking I might perhaps be allowed to look through her clothes.

Juddy. What?

Gerald. No, no. All right. On second thoughts I won't.

JUDDY. I didn't come here for you to insult my wife for me.

GERALD. Didn't you? What did you come here for?

JUDDY. To take that girl away.

GERALD. Where?

JUDDY. To my house.

GERALD. *You'll* take her?

JUDDY. Certainly. I'll wait for her.

GERALD. She's just waiting for a frock.

JUDDY. Oh, well, I'll go and arrange for her to come. You bring her over.

GERALD. Ay, ay, sir. Very likely. Very quickly.

JUDDY. See yer do it then. (*Cross* R. C.) And show a leg. Bustle about.

GERALD. Oh, show a leg and a bustle.

JUDDY. (*Cross up* R. C.) And if yer don't I'll come back and fetch her myself. Day ter yer.

(*Exit, shutting door* R. C.)

(RHODA *appears on balcony.*)

GERALD. Ah! Day ter yer.

RHODA. Well, what did he say?

GERALD. Oh, a lot of nautical nonsense I didn't understand. I think the old rascal likes you rather.

RHODA. Yes, I think he does. (*Coming downstairs to behind settee* L.)

GERALD. Why, do you know him?

RHODA. No, but when I've passed him in the road he's been looky. You know—(*bus.: looking coyly*)—like that.

GERALD. Looky! If he's been looky like that it's off.

Rhoda. What's off? (*Cross in front of settee to* Gerald L. C.)

Gerald. There was an idea you might go there.

Rhoda. Where? To Admiral Juddy's? (*At the bottom of the stairs.*)

Gerald. Yes, and Mrs. Juddy's.

Rhoda. And those horrible Juddy girls?

Gerald. Good Lord! Has he got young?

Rhoda. Oh, please. I couldn't. Those two Miss Juddies would make an awful scandal.

Gerald. Well, you shan't go.

(Rhoda *sits on* L. *of settee.*)

I don't want you to go at all—don't think that.

Rhoda. No. I quite understand.

Gerald. (*Sitting on settee.*) Our little friendship mustn't end here.

Rhoda. Your kind of friendship never ends.

Gerald. Oh, dear, dear, dear! No. Isn't that nice to think of?

Rhoda. (*Looking into* Gerald's *eyes.*) And the same with your cousin.

Gerald. As a matter of fact, I'm very glad he's taking you. He's an awfully simple, soft-hearted chap. He's very fond of canaries. Oh, well, I'll go and tell old Juddy and say you're not coming. (*Leads* Rhoda *across to stairs* L.) Will you be all right? (*Cross* R. *to door up* R.)

Rhoda. Yes. I'll stay in the bedroom. But you don't think my step-father will call again, do you?

Gerald. I hope not. You do like Clive, don't you?

Rhoda. Yes, I think he's awfully nice.

Gerald. Yes—(*pause*)—and I'm a nice little chap too.

(*Exits door* R. C. *to* R. *Close door.*)

(Rhoda *up at window on balcony.* Mrs. Leverett *puts a stealthy head through the kitchen door. She catches sight of* Rhoda, *who is waving to* Gerald, *who is going off round the drive.* Rhoda *calls to* Gerald "Good-bye." Rhoda *wheels round and they see each other.* Mrs. Leverett L. C.)

Rhoda. What are *you* doing here?

Mrs. Leverett. Same to you (*at table* C.), only from last night onward.

Rhoda. (*Anxiously, coming down* L. *behind settee.*) How do you know about that?

Mrs. Leverett. Oh! I've known about it from first thing this morning. And I'm not the only one that knows.

Rhoda. No, in that case I don't suppose you are. (*Cross down stairs to* L.)

Mrs. Leverett. That'll do, miss. (*Turns to* Rhoda.) Impertinence always goes with the other.

Rhoda. (*Hurrying down.*) Come here, please. I want to speak to you.

Mrs. Leverett. (*Moving to* Rhoda, *her temper rising.*) You'll get spoke to all right before long; I'll promise you that.

Rhoda. (*Cross* L. C. *to* Mrs. Leverett). But you weren't told to come back by Mr. Popkiss.

Mrs. Leverett. Him! No. And he'll pop no more of his kisses after this.

Rhoda. What d'you mean?

Mrs. Leverett. You wait and hear what his wife's got to say.

Rhoda. (*Very alarmed.*) His wife?

Mrs. Leverett. Yes. Oh, you can't get away. *I* saw you, this morning. Out you comes on the landing—(*putting on voice. Cross* r.)—"Mr. Popkiss! Mr. Popkiss!" Yes. And back he went to the room, what's more.

Rhoda. Why didn't you speak?

(*Warning for knock.*)

Mrs. Leverett. Oh, I *did* speak.

Rhoda. (*Horrified.*) I can guess. You sneaked to Mrs. Twine.

Mrs. Leverett. Don't you call it sneakin'. That's brazen—(*cross to* Rhoda)—that is—brazen. I know me dooty.

Rhoda. I see. And Mrs. Twine went off to get his wife.

Mrs. Leverett. (*With satisfaction.*) And will shortly be back.

Rhoda. (*Greatly agitated.*) Oh, good heavens!

(*Door knock.*)

(*There is a sharp knock at the front door.* Rhoda *instinctively runs upstairs* l. *She pauses by bedroom door.*)

See who that is.

Mrs. Leverett. (*Looking up at* Rhoda.) You order such about as what is yours to order.

(Rhoda *is half hidden by standing close up to the wall.* Mrs. Leverett *opens front door.*)

(POPPY DICKEY *appears. She is a local maiden in a bright summer frock and carrying a tray of small flags. She laughs a little laugh in two notes, rather like the cry of the cuckoo.*)

POPPY. (*Seeing* MRS. LEVERETT, *she laughs.*) Flags for the Lifeboat ?

MRS. LEVERETT. No, thank you. (*Cross* D. R.)

POPPY. Oh, support our Lifeboat. (*Coming down to her.*)

MRS. LEVERETT. No, thank you. My husband is on board.

POPPY. What about the gentleman who's come here ? Has he got his little flag ?

MRS. LEVERETT. Out.

POPPY. Well, what about the one who's staying with Mrs. Twine ? They said *he* was here. (*Laugh —cuckoo laugh.*)

MRS. LEVERETT. Oh, well, he's not here now, miss.

POPPY. Oh, how too crushing of him ! No little flags at all ? Well, good morning. P'r'aps I'll meet one of the gentlemen in the road.

(*Exits* R. C., *and* MRS. LEVERETT *closes the door.*)

MRS. LEVERETT. (*At door.*) P'r'aps you will. (*Cross to* C. *behind table and look towards door* R. C.) And it wouldn't be the first time you've done *that* !

(*She returns to kitchen. Closes door.*)

(RHODA *immediately runs down to door* R. C. *She opens it and runs a few yards out in front drive.*)

RHODA. (*Calling in a guarded voice.*) I say! I say! Come here! (*Cross* D. R. C.)

(POPPY *reappears, looking extremely surprised and intrigued.* RHODA *beckons her in.* POPPY *enters wide-eyed. She crosses* D. R.)

POPPY. (*Taking stock of her.*) Well, it takes a good deal to surprise me.

RHODA. I know you by sight. You live in Chumpton, don't you?

POPPY. That's right. My name's Poppy Dickey. I've heard about you too. But what's *this* little episode?

RHODA. Oh, do be kind and help me.

POPPY. But I'm selling flags for the Lifeboat. I'd love to know what *you're* doing!

RHODA. I simply *had* to come here. (*Close door* R. C.)

POPPY. Why? Did you know these boys before?

RHODA. No. But I came in here last night.

POPPY. What, and said " Oh, I simply had to come "—like that?

RHODA. No. Well—I came here because—there was nothing else to do.

POPPY. (*Breezily.*) Really? (*Cross to front of table.*) That's what I call a good reason but a bad excuse.

RHODA. Listen, please. (*Glances at kitchen door, then speaks intensely.*) I'm in great trouble.

POPPY. I'm not surprised. I've asked for a bit of trouble myself before now, but I've never chased it quite as hard as this.

RHODA. Let me tell you. I had a row at home. So I came here.

POPPY. Last night, this was?

RHODA. Yes.

POPPY. And met these boys?

RHODA. Yes.

POPPY. And you've stayed here?

RHODA. Yes, I've had to.

POPPY. Like you are now?

RHODA. Yes, more or less.

POPPY. All night and ever since?

RHODA. Yes.

POPPY. Think of that! And me selling flags!

RHODA. But I do want help. (*Very distressed.*)

POPPY. You don't strike me as wanting much help.

RHODA. I do. Terribly. Oh, stay and help me! There may be trouble. That's why I want your help.

POPPY. (*Crosses to settee.*) Well, I like that. If I didn't have a hand in the crime I don't see getting stung for the inquest. (*Sits on arm of settee down stage.*)

RHODA. (*Cross to settee, kneels.*) Listen. Lend me that frock for ten minutes and I shall be saved.

POPPY. Really? And what'll *I* be?

RHODA. Those two will be back directly. You wait in that bedroom and tell them.

POPPY. (*Rise*). Me wait in that bedroom with no frock on for the two boys?

RHODA. Yes. Oh, it would be wonderful if you would!

(POPPY *laughs.*)

(*Imploringly—rising.*) You'll do it?

POPPY. Well, it's a bit out of the usual. But I can see you're in trouble.

(*Warning for knock at door.*)

(*Hesitating.*) Yes, but—(*cross to lower end of settee*) —you're sure these boys will enter into the spirit of the thing?

RHODA. Of course. They're darlings. (*Laughs.*) You'll be doing *them* a good turn too.

POPPY. Yes, but it's me I'm thinking of.

RHODA. Well, you too. Because, you see, you can sell them flags for the Lifeboat.

POPPY. (*With her cuckoo laugh.*) Strikes me, I *am* the lifeboat. (*She turns, goes upstairs, with* RHODA *following. Halts half-way up.*) But if I do this, you will bring back my frock?

RHODA. Yes, yes. I promise I will. Immediately.

POPPY. Righto. (*Cross upstairs* L.) You needn't overdo it. I dare say *fairly* quickly will do.

(*A loud knock at the front door.* RHODA *hustles* POPPY *into bedroom* L.)

RHODA. Look out. Come on. In here. Quick!

(*She gets* POPPY *into bedroom as* MRS. LEVERETT *enters from kitchen.*)
(RHODA *pretends to be looking out of bedroom.*)

There's somebody at the front door.

MRS. LEVERETT. You kindly keep your orders for such as is theirs to get. My name is not Nutts.

(RHODA *goes into bedroom.*)

(MRS. LEVERETT *goes and opens front door.* TWINE *is waiting outside. He is startled to see* MRS. LEVERETT, *and much embarrassed.*)

TWINE. Oh! (*Steps inside.*)

MRS. LEVERETT. Well, sir?

TWINE. Well?

MRS. LEVERETT. Well? (*Brief pause.*) WELL?

TWINE. I—I didn't expect to see *you.*

MRS. LEVERETT. Why not?

TWINE. I didn't think you were here.

MRS. LEVERETT. Why shouldn't I be here, sir?

TWINE. Oh! For no reason I know of.

(*During these lines* TWINE *moves down* R., MRS. LEVERETT *follows.*)

MRS. LEVERETT. Then why didn't you expect to see me?

TWINE. I don't know exactly.

MRS. LEVERETT. You knew I was working here, didn't you?

TWINE. Yes, dear.

MRS. LEVERETT. What!

TWINE. I beg your pardon. I mean yes.

MRS. LEVERETT. Well, then?

TWINE. Mr. Popkiss told me you'd gone.

MRS. LEVERETT. Oh! Then have *you* been here this morning?

TWINE. (*Cross to* R. C.) Oh! No—I—I met him out.

MRS. LEVERETT. Ah! Just now when he went out? (*Cross to* TWINE R. C.)

TWINE. (*Gladly.*) Yes.

MRS. LEVERETT. (*With triumph.*) Then if you

met him just now, who did you come here expecting to see?

TWINE. Oh! I came—(*with an inspiration*)—about a bag I lost.

MRS. LEVERETT. Where?

TWINE. Here.

MRS. LEVERETT. When?

TWINE. Oh! No, I didn't lose it. (*Crosses to* C. *front of table.*) He lost it. I want to know if it's come back.

MRS. LEVERETT. Come back from where? (*Following* TWINE C.)

TWINE. From wherever it went to.

MRS. LEVERETT. You said it went here.

TWINE. Oh!

MRS. LEVERETT. (*Peering at him suspiciously.*) Mr. Twine!

TWINE. What?

MRS. LEVERETT. Do you know anything?

TWINE. (*Very nervously.*) Know?

MRS. LEVERETT. Yes—know.

TWINE. No.

MRS. LEVERETT. No?

TWINE. Yes. No. Really. It's all right about the bag. Don't mention it. (*He turns tail and goes between table and* MRS. LEVERETT.) (*Exit* R. C.)

(MRS. LEVERETT *follows him into porch and stands staring after him and shaking her head suspiciously.*)

(RHODA *in* POPPY DICKEY'S *dress nips out of the bedroom—glances into the hall, then goes quickly down the stairs, having ascertained that* MRS. LEVERETT *is in the porch; exit door down* L.)

(*As* MRS. LEVERETT *returns to* L. *of table,* TWINE *again enters* R. C. *and comes down very stealthily to* R. *of table.*)

Mrs. Leverett——

MRS. LEVERETT. (*Very startled.*) Oh, well, what now, sir?

TWINE. (*Moving towards her* C. *front of table.*) You said something about—did I know? Tell me, do you know something? (*Very close to* MRS. LEVERETT.)

MRS. LEVERETT. Do I know what?

TWINE. Oh! I don't know—I'm sure I don't know.

MRS. LEVERETT. Do I know what you don't know?

TWINE. (*Gladly.*) Yes.

MRS. LEVERETT. Well, if you don't know what you know, how do I know if I know it?

TWINE. (*Turning* R. *towards door* R. C.) Oh, I think I'll get out. (*Turns* R.) Oh dear!—(*in fear*)—here comes Mr. Popkiss back.

MRS. LEVERETT. Oh, does he! I've had enough of him to-day. I'm going back to my kitchen.

(*Exit* D. L.)

(TWINE *tries to sneak out* D. L. GERALD *enters and stops him.*)

GERALD. Hallo, Harold!

TWINE. Oh, blow!

GERALD. What's the meaning of this?

TWINE. Of what?

GERALD. Of this. This—this. You know what *this* means, don't you ?

TWINE. Yes.

GERALD. Well, what's the meaning of this ?

TWINE. I don't know.

GERALD. You told Admiral Thing !

TWINE. I had to.

GERALD. You swore you wouldn't.

TWINE. I couldn't help it.

GERALD. You broke a swear. That's one thing a gentleman never breaks.

TWINE. I don't think anything will matter now. (*Look over* L.) That woman's back in the kitchen.

GERALD. What ! Why not say so ? (*Crossing to door* D. L. *quickly and calling in.*) Where are you ? No, not you, cat. (*To imaginary cat.*) The other one.

TWINE. Isn't she there ?

GERALD. No. What's the meaning of this ?

TWINE. (*Annoyed.*) Don't keep asking me *that.*

GERALD. I didn't say *that* ; I said *this.*

TWINE. I don't even know what you mean by *this.*

GERALD. Come, come, Harold. That's what I was asking *you.*

(*Enter* CLIVE R. C. *from* L., *running, with very small parcel, which he puts on the table.*)

CLIVE. Here you are. I told you I'd get it.

GERALD. A frock ?

CLIVE. Yes. And everything else.

TWINE. But what about Gertrude's bag ?

GERALD. Well, go and get it back from Putz.

TWINE. I won't.

GERALD. You won't?

CLIVE. But you gave it to Putz.

GERALD. Well, get out of this, anyhow. We don't like your trousers or your face.

TWINE. Blow you both. (*Cross up* R.) I beg your pardon, but really you make me lose my temper.

(*Goes off* R. C. *to* L.)

CLIVE. I'll take these things up to Rhoda.

GERALD. No. *I* will. (*Taking parcel.*) *I* shall only go as far as the door. (*Going upstairs.*)

TWINE. (*Rushing back* R. C.) Quick! Look out! Something appalling.

GERALD. (*Halting on stairs.*) Then don't bring it in here.

CLIVE. What is it?

TWINE. Gertrude, Clara, and mother. And the daily woman at the gate.

GERALD. Clara! (*He comes downstairs again and throws away parcel.*)

CLIVE. Treason. Somebody's done the dirty.

GERALD. You swine of a Twine.

TWINE. No; it's Gertrude. But don't say I said so. Good-bye, you fellows. (*Hurries out through kitchen door* L.) Good-bye.

(*Exit.*)

GERALD. Clive! What'll I do? What'll I say?

CLIVE. Show her the girl.

GERALD. But her mind's been poisoned by Gertrude.

CLIVE. Show her the girl. That's enough for anyone.

(*Enter* CLARA R. C., *cross* D. R. C.)

GERALD. Clara! Darling!

(MRS. POSSETT, GERTRUDE, *and* MRS. LEVERETT *enter* R. C. *from* L. *They go to settee.*)

CLARA. Oh, Gerald, if there were anything wrong, could you kiss me like that?

GERALD. Of course I could, darling.

CLIVE. Couldn't, you fool.

GERALD. Couldn't, you fool. Couldn't, darling. (*Turns.*) You needn't sit down all over the place. I want to speak to Clara.

CLIVE. Yes, alone.

GERTRUDE. Certainly not.

CLARA. Thank you, Gertrude. I prefer to speak to him alone. (*Cross* L. C.)

GERTRUDE. Mrs. Leverett, is that girl still here?

MRS. LEVERETT. She is. In the bedroom.

GERTRUDE. There.

CLARA. She *is* still here?

MRS. POSSETT. I feel sick.

CLIVE. Oh, stop that. (*To* MRS. POSSETT.) There's quite enough on hand without that.

GERTRUDE. Mrs. Leverett, take my mother to the drawing-room.

GERALD. That'll be nice for the drawing-room.

MRS. LEVERETT. (*Helping* MRS. POSSETT.) I didn't come here for that.

CLIVE. No, but she *did*. Take her away.

MRS. LEVERETT. I came here to say my say, and say my say I mean to do.

(*Exit with* MRS. POSSETT R. *to drawing-room.*)

CLARA. (*To* GERALD.) Now, perhaps you'll tell me why that girl's still here.

CLIVE. Go on, the gong's gone

GERALD. (*Cross to* CLARA.) Certainly. I'm very glad she is. (*To* CLIVE.) Am I?

CLIVE. Delighted!

GERALD. There you are. I'm delighted. She came here last night—poor little soul—alone in pyjamas. In pyjamas alone. Driven from home. Driven by Putz.

GERTRUDE. Rubbish! She's a notorious girl.

CLIVE. She's the sweetest little girl I've ever seen.

GERALD. She's certainly the sweetest *I've* ever seen—almost.

CLIVE. I tell you she's above suspicion.

GERALD. Yes. Like Potiphar's wife.

CLIVE. She radiates purity and innocence.

CLARA. Well, I haven't accused. I'll see her and judge.

CLIVE. Yes, go on. Call her out of that room.

GERALD. (*Boldly.*) Quite right. (*Calls.*) Little girl. Come out of that room.

(*They all look up at bedroom, with their backs to audience.*)

CLIVE. Now you shall see.

(POPPY DICKEY *enters in cami-knickers from bedroom on balcony* L.; *crosses to the other end of the balcony, singing and dancing.*)

POPPY. "Oh, sir, she's my baby—
Yes, sir, she's my baby;
Oh, sir, she's my baby now!"

(*She turns to look over front of balcony; as she*

does so she calls out, "Flags for the Lifeboat!" *Realising the situation, she gives a scream and rushes back into bedroom* L. GERALD *and* CLIVE *turn to each other, looking thunderstruck.*)

GERTRUDE. What's the meaning of this?

GERALD. Don't ask me.

CLARA. Is *that* the girl?

GERALD. No, it isn't.

CLARA. Then who is it?

GERALD. (*To* CLIVE.) Who is it?

CLIVE. I didn't put it there.

GERALD. Some mistake, darling.

CLARA. Rubbish! You said "Come out," and out she came.

GERALD. Yes; but this wasn't the one we wanted to come out.

GERTRUDE. That's another local girl—she's one of the Dickeys.

GERALD. (*To* CLIVE.) You hear that! She's one of the Dickeys.

CLIVE. Yes, she looks it.

(POPPY *re-enters from bedroom wearing* RHODA'S *dressing-gown.*)

GERTRUDE. They've evidently been collecting all the fast girls of the place.

POPPY. (*Above.*) Don't you start on me, Mrs. Twine.

GERTRUDE. (*Crosses stairs.*) Where's that girl from up the road? Is she there too?

POPPY. I don't know anything about any girl from up any road.

GERALD. (*To* CLIVE.) What happened ?

CLIVE. Don't ask silly questions. I'm not a wizard.

GERALD. Somebody is.

GERTRUDE. Why did you come here ?

POPPY. I came selling flags, and I went upstairs to mend my frock. I caught it on the gatepost.

GERALD. Is this friend or foe ?

CLARA. It's all a pack of lies. I know that.

(GERTRUDE *goes upstairs.*)

GERALD. Oh, darling—not a whole pack.

POPPY. (*To* GERTRUDE.) Where are you going ? That's *my* room.

(*They exit into bedroom up* L.)

CLARA. There you are. *Her* room.

CLIVE. Yes, but the other bedrooms is elsewhere.

GERTRUDE. (*Off.*) Just as I thought.

POPPY. (*Off.*) Mind your own business.

GERTRUDE. (*Enters.*) There's not a sign of a frock in that room.

(POPPY *enters from bedroom* L. *on balcony.*)

CLARA. Then this is the one that was here all night.

GERALD. No, darling. I keep telling you. A much better one than that. The other one radiates purity. Nothing like this Dickey thing at all.

POPPY. Well, you're a nice one to try and help.

GERALD. You think you're helping me ?

CLIVE. Of course she is. A jolly fine effort. Well tried, Miss Flags.

POPPY. Thank you. I'm glad someone's got a glad hand.

Gertrude. It's quite clear. You were to stay here and tell lies while the other little wretch escaped. Go into that room. I'll tell your mother.

Poppy. You try. Mother's a sport, and she hates you like hell.

(*Exit into bedroom on balcony* L.)

Clara. I see. There are two of them.

(Gertrude *crosses behind table.*)

Gerald. That's right.

Clara. One each.

Gerald. That's right. No, there aren't two. Well, yes, there are two—but—— (*To* Clive). Go on. Can't you say something?

Clara. Why are there two ?

Gerald. (*To* Clive.) Why are there two? That's you.

Clive. Now get this, Clara. For some reason, about which we're a trifle hazy, there are two—namely, radiates purity and Flags for the Lifeboat.

Gertrude. And one's as bad as the other.

Gerald. No ; she's worse.

Clive. We've never set eyes on this Dickey thing—neither of us. I don't quite know why *I* haven't—

(Gerald *digs* Clive, *drawing his attention to the fact that* Gertrude *is eyeing him suspiciously.*)

—but there it is.

Gertrude. (*Crosses to* R. C. *from behind table.*) If it wasn't all some intrigue, why didn't you ask for my help last night ?

Clive. I'll tell you that. Because you're a jealous, green-eyed, backbiting woman.

Gerald. Thank you, Clive.

Clive. That's all right. She's got some more to come. (*Then to* Gertrude.) You're very fond of calling other people liars—but what about you, with your vile scandals and venomous libels and dirty little tattling tea-parties?

Gertrude. You'll gain nothing by rudeness.

Clive. I don't care whether I gain or not. It's well overdue to you. (*Turns to* Clara.) And, Clara, don't you accuse Gerald. The girl he's defending is the victim of a wicked scandal. So long as Gertrude can find some mud to fling she doesn't care a damn whether it sticks.

Gerald. Quite right.

Gertrude. You needn't lose your temper. Just because you arranged for the girl to be here last night and then weren't allowed to stay here yourself too.

(*Goes into drawing-room* R.)

Clive. That woman's got a mind like a very ingenious sink.

(Clara *crosses* R. C.)

Gerald. Clara darling. Don't go.

Clara. Oh, I know it's true what she says. You're only trying to deceive me.

Gerald. No, I'm trying not to.

(Clara *exits up* R.)

Clive. Look here—we must play our trump card, that's all.

GERALD. Have we got one?

CLIVE. Yes, I'm going along to that house.

GERALD. No, don't risk bringing Rhoda back. She's too pretty. She wouldn't go well. I know she wouldn't.

CLIVE. No, no, I don't mean her. I'm going to get Putz.

GERALD. Putz?

CLIVE. Yes. I'm going to get a big boulder and fling it in the pit of Putz's stomach and run like hell with him after me.

GERALD. Fine, Clive!—that's fine! That'll show Clara. Infuriate him. Don't throw stones, throw wurts.

CLIVE. (*Going.*) All right Oh, if you can, Gerald, have that cat handy——

GERALD. Why?

CLIVE. Because with any luck I'll bring Conrad too.

(CLIVE *goes hurriedly up* R. C.)

(GERALD *takes thought, then he picks up the parcel that* CLIVE *gave him with the dress, and makes for the stairs.*)

(*There are sounds of dissension in the drawing-room and* CLARA *returns. She speaks as she enters.*)

CLARA. (*Entering from* R. *and saying as she enters.*) Quite enough to stand without that.

GERALD. (*Running down the stairs with the parcel behind him, hiding it from* CLARA.) What's the matter, darling?

CLARA. I wasn't speaking to you.

GERALD. Oh! you sounded so cross, I thought you were.

CLARA. It's Gertrude. You can't even misbehave yourself without Gertrude finding it out.

GERALD. No, I know I can't. Nobody can.

CLARA. Then you *did* misbehave yourself?

GERALD. You don't believe that, do you?

CLARA. I hate to. But a girl coming in here with pyjamas on. (*Looking away.*)

GERALD. I know, dear. I didn't want her to have them on.

CLARA. What!

GERALD. I mean I'd rather she'd been wearing a hat.

CLARA. Oh, be honest with me. I'm trying to be loyal and loving.

GERALD. I know you are, darling, and I'm trying to explain it away—to explain, I mean—without the away.

CLARA. I don't think you need try to tell me any more.

GERALD. Thank you, darling. (*Attempting to embrace her.*)

CLARA. No. (*Pushing* GERALD *away gently.*) You admit to keeping the girl here all night?

GERALD. No, dear, letting her stay here all night. That's all the difference. Think of this poor little girl. She came here last night through the long and dewy grass. She was soused—I mean soaked.

CLARA. I don't care.

GERALD. But you must care—the poor little soul, she was cold. Her poor little toes were rattling like dominoes. Her trousers were wet up to the knee, so what did I do? I gave her mine.

CLARA. Your trousers?

GERALD. Yes, my spare bedwear pair. I couldn't turn her out again into the dark and dewy night.

CLARA. Why not?

GERALD. Why, I didn't want mine wet as well.

CLARA. Why did she leave home?

GERALD. Why, think of her home-life with only this man and Mrs. Nutts. A great, big brute of a step-father stepping all over the place. A bully of a man cracking a whip, cracking her and cracking Nutts. Oh, think of it—a poor little child in distress, a life in peril. I said I must save her. Clara would wish it, so I saved her till this morning.

CLARA. It sounds a very unlikely story.

GERALD. Yes, that is what I told Clive.

(GERTRUDE *entering from drawing-room.* GERALD *crosses* L. *of table to* C.)

GERTRUDE. Clara, I must see you about a room for mother.

(CLIVE *comes hurrying back* R. C. *Crosses* L. C. *to* GERALD.)

CLIVE. One moment. Look out! (*To* CLARA.) There's someone here I want you to see.

GERALD. (*To* CLIVE.) Putz?

CLIVE. Yes.

GERALD. Is he all right?

CLIVE. (*With a nod.*) Livid with fury. (*To* CLARA.) Now, listen, Clara. You've got to be told about this man—the step-father.

GERTRUDE. He's not her step-father at all.

CLIVE. You shall judge that when you see him.

GERALD. Yes, and once you've seen him you won't want to see her.

CLIVE. No. You'd help to save any girl from a devil like that.

GERALD. He's a monster—a fiend in human shape.

CLIVE. A violent, savage swine.

GERALD. Without respect for God or man. You wait and see!

(PUTZ *appears in the doorway; he knocks loudly, a double rap.*)

(*Seeing Putz.*) This is the man.

(CLARA *crosses* D. L.)

Yes, come in.

(PUTZ *comes down* R. C.)

And say your worst.

PUTZ. (*Cross behind table, speaking very gently.*) Zee worst? Ah, nein—I want to say you something nice. It is now aller right.

GERALD. It doesn't look all right to me.

CLIVE. (*Cross* R. *to* PUTZ.) No, certainly not. Look here! If you can't misbehave yourself properly you'd better get out of this.

GERTRUDE. (*To* PUTZ.) Will you kindly say what happened last night?

PUTZ. (*Crosses* D. R.) They try to take her from me. Aller der night she stay away from me. But I forgive her. Und I forgive you, my dear frent, absolute. (*Cross* C. *in front of table to* GERALD.)

Clive. (*To* Putz.) You liar! (*To* Gerald.) This is no good. (*Behind table* R. C.)

Gerald. No. Go on. Infuriate him—wurts!

Clive. (*Cross to* Putz, *who is* R. C. *in front of table.*) If you don't send her straight back here I'll come and fetch her. Come on. You come with me now.

Putz. Wait, please. I wish for peace. (*Goes up to chair.*)

Clara. Is this the fiend in human shape?

Gerald. He's the wrong shape to-day.

Putz. (*Coming down* R. C.) Look, please. The trunk and the hud.

Gertrude. (*Seizing hat.*) What's the meaning of this outrage?

Clive. (*Cross* L. C. *in front of table.*) Clara! You mustn't believe this lying German humbug.

Clara. I believe my own eyes and ears!

Gerald. Yes, but you can't believe his nose and mouth.

Clara. He's the quietest man I've ever seen.

Gerald. Don't go, Clara!

Clara. No. One hour apart from me and back you go.

Gerald. Back where?

Clara. Back to your old life with Clive.

Rhoda				
o	Putz	Clive	Gerald	Clara
	o	o	o	o

Gerald. It's Bognor again.

(*Enter* Rhoda, *cross down* R.)

Clive. Look out! Here she is!

(*Rhoda is in her own clothes—outdoor costume.*)

Clara. Is this the girl?

Gerald. Yes. But don't be misled. She doesn't look nearly so nice in pyjamas.

Clara. She certainly doesn't look what Gertrude says.

Rhoda. I'm not. But your husband's been tremendously kind to me all the same.

Gerald. Oh, not tremendously—just kind.

(*Enter* Mrs. Leverett r.)

Mrs. Leverett. Well, I've finished this job.

Clive. (*To* Gerald.) Hold on. I see a ray. (*Cross to* r. Mrs. Leverett.) You, Mrs. Flanagan—that was a deliberate untruth you told me last night!

Mrs. Leverett. Me? How dare you! and what do you mean?

Clive. (*Pointing to* Putz.) You told me this little girl and this man Putz were living in sin.

Putz. (*Changing his manner quickly.*) Was is das? (*Fiercely.*) What you make?

(Gerald *crosses up* l. *of table to* r. c.)

Gerald. That's an awful thing to say.

Putz. Who shall say of her?

Clive. (*Bringing* Mrs. Leverett *forward.*) Come on. Ask *her*.

Putz. (*Cross* r. *furiously to* Mrs. Leverett.) You are who?

Mrs. Leverett. I only said I'd always heard. (*Cross to other side of* Putz l.)

Putz. You are who to say of her and Rhoda——

Mrs. Leverett. Mrs. Twine told me——

GERALD. (*Pushes* MRS. TWINE *forward to* PUTZ—L. *of* PUTZ.) This is Mrs. Twine.

GERTRUDE. Gerald, how dare you?

PUTZ. (*Wheeling on* GERTRUDE.) Herr Gott! you shall say of my step-daughter that she is not *so* gut. *Allerferdampter—Schwein—verfluchter Cammail!*

(*During this speech he forces* MRS. TWINE *and* MRS. LEVERETT *over and backwards* L. GERALD *and* CLIVE *follow behind* PUTZ *to* L. C.)

(PUTZ *turns back and clears his way between* CLIVE *and* GERALD. *Finally, he picks up the bag of clothes and flings it to the ground, and with a final roar of anger*——

(*Exits* R. C.)

Kreutz! Himmel!! Donnerwetter!!!

Pronounced: Croyts, Himmell, Donner-vetter.
(*Cross, Heaven, Thunder-weather.*)

(*At* PUTZ'S *outburst* CLARA *has instinctively gone to* GERALD *for protection and* RHODA *to* CLIVE.)

FIRST CURTAIN.

(SECOND CURTAIN: RHODA *is in* CLIVE'S *arms and* CLARA *in* GERALD'S. *Unseen,* CLIVE *and* GERALD, *who are standing back to back, shake hands,* CLIVE'S L. *hand and* GERALD'S R., *with their eyes still on* RHODA *and* CLARA.)

CURTAIN.

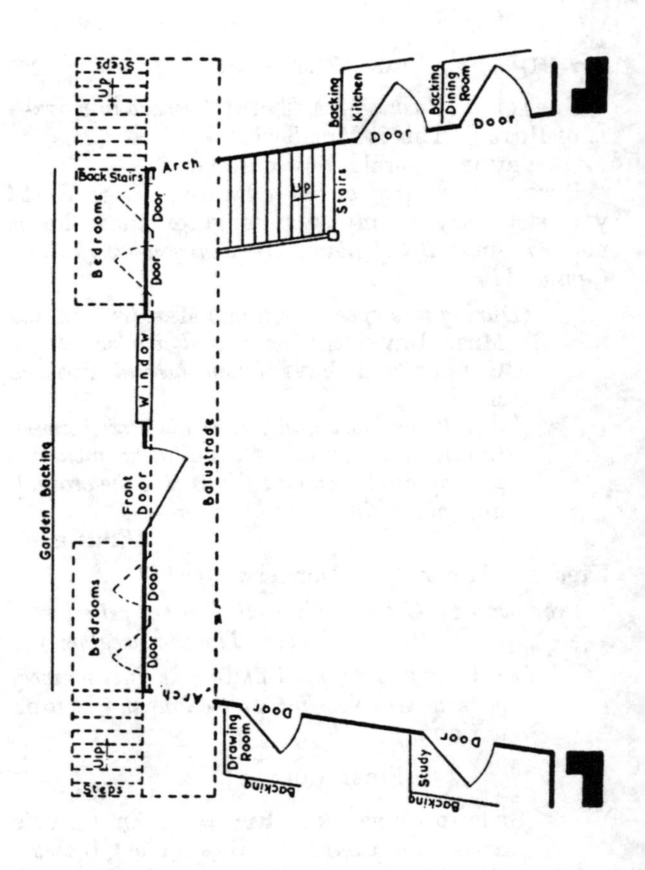

PRINTED IN GREAT BRITAIN BY
THE LONGDUNN PRESS LTD., BRISTOL.